Being in Child Care

A Journey into Self

Being in Child Care

A Journey into Self

Gerry Fewster

Routledge
Taylor & Francis Group
New York   London

Being in Child Care: A Journey into Self has also been published as *Child & Youth Services*, Volume 14, Number 2 1990.

First published by

The Haworth Press, Inc., 10 Alice Street, Binghamton, NY 13904-1580
EUROSPAN/Haworth, 3 Henrietta Street, London WC2E 8LU England

This edition published 2012 by Routledge

Routledge
Taylor & Francis Group
711 Third Avenue
New York, NY 10017

Routledge
Taylor & Francis Group
27 Church Road
Hove East Sussex BN3 2FA

Library of Congress Cataloging-in-Publication Data

Being in child care : a journey into self / Gerry Fewster.
    p. cm.
    ''Being in child care: a journey into self has also been published in Child & youth services, volume 14, number 2, 1990''—T.p. verso.
    Includes bibliographical references.
    ISBN 0-86656-979-0 (alk. paper) :
    1. Child care workers—United States. 2. Child care—United States. I. Title.
HV851.F49   1990
362.7'12—dc20
                                                       90-33937
                                                       CIP

To Judith

Being in Child Care

A Journey into Self

CONTENTS

ABOUT THE AUTHOR

Gerry Fewster, PhD, is Executive Director of William Roper Hull Child and Family Services in Calgary, Alberta, Canada. He is Adjunct Associate Professor in the Department of Educational Psychology at the University of Calgary and editor of the *Journal of Child and Youth Care*.

PREFACE

Reflections Upon Reflections

In the face of the continual demands of young people in care for various kinds of our attention, only rarely do we have time to sit back to think about what we do and why. Preparation for child and youth care workers tends likewise to emphasize the concrete: techniques that "work" (perhaps in the sense of allowing us to manage or manipulate behavior); policies that need to be implemented; standards that need to be maintained; skills that need to be taught; etc. In their proper place, each of these is important, and available time usually does not permit us to teach as much about them as good workers need to know. Yet in any proportion, these do not in themselves add up to effective child and youth care work.

Why then, have we focused so heavily on them? In part, this seems to me to be another reflection of the crisis-management orientation of our traditionally overworked, understaffed, undertrained endeavour to meet needs for which available resources are inadequate. But even more importantly, it reflects our despair about the possibility of teaching the more fundamental essence of what we are about other than through direct experience. Yet given the high turnover rate characteristic of the field, we cannot afford the full year of experience that many feel is required for someone to gain the facility needed to perform the work well. Perhaps 80% of our personnel are gone by then; perhaps that would not be the case if they could learn the job more quickly.

Thus, we can ill-afford the somewhat smug anti-intellectual stance that has characterized many of our colleagues, who prefer the more romantic notion that the "truth" is accessible only to the few barefooted "naturals" among us to whom it has been revealed. Yet we have had little in the way of professional literature or text material with which to counter their views. Most of our literature has been either academic or experiential, either lectures or stories, rarely combining these two elements in the way it must — in tandem, of course, with field experience — if learning effective practice is to occur systematically and within a reasonable time frame.

Although I have not tested it in the classroom or in practice settings, this is what it appears to me that Gerry Fewster's latest work will enable us to do. It is a story, but one that challenges the reader to understand and internalize from his or her own experience. It represents a particular point of view, as any such experiential approach must, but one that seems increasingly generic as one works his or her way through it. Most important, it gets to the heart of child and youth care practice as it focuses on the relationship between worker and client and on the roots of that relationship in the worker's own experience and development. Thus, it provides a superstructure upon which the kinds of more specific knowledge and understanding referred to above can be built and integrated.

This book does not lily-coat the intensity and pain of child and youth care work, nor does it spare the reader from sharing in the suffering that too often afflicts our clients, but it also highlights the growth and satisfaction that await those who find this work to be their calling. It should serve us all by helping those whom the requirements of the field do not fit to screen themselves out, and by bringing into the work those who will be less likely to depart as soon as so many do today. Thus, and in the hands of capable, sensitive teachers and supervisors, it should do much to enhance our work in the service of personal development for the young people in our care, as well as for those who choose to work with them.

Jerome Beker

Introduction

Calgary
Alberta
Canada

July 3, 1988

Dear Charlotte,

It has been a long time. The rose is for the summer in Vermont. The manuscript is for your love — and your comments.

I still think about our personal 'workshop'; the decisions we made and the separate paths we chose — me to transform children's services and you to follow your dream of a Child Care profession. I wonder where your dream is now?

In those days Child Care was its own child, innocently moving out into the world without fear or pretense. Those of us who nurtured, talked of a 'new era,' a 'professional metamorphis,' and even the beginnings of a 'child-centered society.' There was an energy and excitement, unprecedented in the ponderous environs of the helping services. Across the continent, masses of young people joined the ranks, letting the world know they cared. They were curious, asking questions and looking for answers. I remember your fears about the kinds of answers they would get and the channels that would be used to draw off their energy. I also remember your own commitment to offer support and protection, not as a patronizing 'advocate,' but as a child care practitioner. Your other professional certificates are still in the drawer where you left them. I wonder where your dream is now?

My own experience has not been encouraging. Now when I attend local, national, or even international child care conferences, I see the same faces and hear the same ideas about practice and exhortations about 'professionalism.' As you know, few of the 'stars' have actually emerged from the ranks of Child Care. Every issue of the *Journal of Child Care* that I edit represents a struggle to draw out articles that actually reflect the reality of working with children. The direct experience of practitioners is rarely shared. At the regional level it seems to me that many of the Associations, designed to create forums for developmental issues, have become more like Unions concerned with the survival of a marginal profession at the lowest point on the professional totem. Your fear that child care workers might become the pawns of other professionals has a place in my reality. My fear is that Child and Youth Care, in general, might have lost touch with its own sense of destiny.

And yet, my dear Charlotte, there are more child care practitioners in more places than ever before. There are undergraduate and graduate programs at two major universities, conferences are well attended, and four journals offer opportunities for people to speak with each other. There must be many places, other than Willoughby House, where Child and Youth Care has established its own developmental pattern. There must be many teachers, other than yourself, who work with direct experience rather than with the worn out tools of those who went before. I want to believe that, in the contact-boundary area where youngsters and adults encounter each other, we can still find energy and learning.

Of course, I want you to tell me that your dream is unfolding through the experience of each day. I want you to assure me that the spirit of your beloved Child Care is still alive, and that the visions and hopes we shared have not been reduced to the level of a Don Quixote romance. You see, unlike you Charlotte, I still hang on to a delusion that the world can, and should, mould itself around my idealistic pictures. On reflection, I think that this was why we chose different pathways. Now, regardless of my romantic needs and aspirations, I know that you will respond to my enquiries — and the manuscript — from a perspective that is distinctly yours. I look forward to that.

Love,

Gerry

Los Angeles
California
U.S.A.

July 8, 1988

Dear Gerry,

A single rose, memories of a summer in Vermont, and a manuscript. The combination of these things is so uniquely and delight-
fully you. I do miss your spirit and your support. I will read the Ms.
over the weekend and offer my comments to you in writing before
the end of next week — unless you would like to come down here for
a more personal exchange. For the moment, let me respond to the
questions posed in your letter.

Your picture of Child and Youth Care is not strange to me, but
yes, I do maintain curiosity and excitement about its evolution. In
my picture, what you so clearly describe is a stage of growth, although I must confess to some frustration in waiting for the next
stumble forward. Perhaps it will be a leap of faith rather than conscious step. I say this because, like you, I believe that this profession lacks the sense of cohesion and identity to create a vision of its
own destiny. Meanwhile it is indeed a pawn for those who seem to
know what they want. Politicians and policy makers who want ex-
pedient window dressing, administrators and program planners
looking for cheap mobile labour, professionals searching for ways
to plug the gaps of their own practices and, unfortunately, a general
public in a constant search for someone to hold 'responsible' — they
all use Child and Youth Care for their own ends.

In saying this you, of all people, know that I am not trying to
create an illusion of victims and villains. Developmentally, Child
and Youth Care is exactly where it should be. Where I would like it
to be is another issue. Meanwhile my own contribution keeps me
fully occupied and committed. I liked your metaphor of the profession being "its own child" in those early years. Now we seem to be
dealing with a compliant pre-adolescent, fragmented in identity and
unsure in purpose.

In my own work I focus upon the validation of experience as a foundation for security and growth. In other words, I am encouraging practitioners to examine and trust what they learn from their day-to-day encounters with young people. At Willoughby House we are building some interesting new perspectives this way. There is excitement, anticipation and wonderful energy in this process, Gerry — come and check it out for yourself.

Ultimately, the future of my chosen profession will depend upon the individual and collective decisions of my colleagues in the 'trenches.' It is my belief that, during this developmental lull, they are building the experience and insight necessary to move on to the next phase. Child and Youth Care is so extensive and pervasive that its presence can't be denied or diminished. The term "sleeping giant" was coined at the first Canadian National Conference in 1981. While the assumption that the slumbering ogre has "awakened" might have been premature at that time, I suggest that 'she' is now beginning to stir.

While we might be on the verge of another phase of growth, the visions that will mould the future are already forming in the hearts and minds of this generation of youngsters, many of whom will have had direct experience with child care workers. It will be their experience, their perceptions, and their beliefs that will determine how we attend to the needs of children in the years to come. When I look at my own place in all of this, the focus becomes clear and the task becomes manageable. By inviting other practitioners to examine and share their own experience, I know that they generate the information that feeds the insatiable curiosity of the children who work with them. Here we find our humanity, our individuality and our connectedness. Deep inside I know that children who grow up in the presence of such people will find a way to learn and to love. I also know that, through encouraging others, I find my own learning and loving.

For some reason, my dear friend, I find these things so easy to say to you. But now I want to know about your life in the enchanted forest of service delivery. Let me turn the questions back on you. I have a fantasy that you are moving back to Child Care, but this may be my wishful way of reading between the lines. The prospect of sharing the road with you again is incredible for me. Perhaps the manuscript will give me some more clues. Meanwhile, please address my curiosity on the other questions. I really miss your presence.

Love,

Charlotte

Taking Another Look

Paul's questions were turning into self doubts as he slipped into the supervisor's office and eased himself into one of the well seasoned armchairs that surrounded a long suffering coffee table. The space around was unremarkable but comfortably personal; it seemed to welcome him gently and without judgement. The only light came from a lamp suspended low over the table, its parchment shade reluctantly allowing a diffused mellow glow to circle the chairs and evaporate into the darkness beyond.

He peered out into the gloom hoping to assemble more information about the woman who had replied to his letter. A long oak table, serving as a desk, stood out against the corrugation of heavy curtains that, drawn against the blackness of the night, covered the entire wall behind. The whole arrangement was orderly — almost stately he thought. A brass reading lamp, telephone, writing pad and appointment book, functionally located; a straight backed wooden chair with velvet upholstery, squarely positioned; an electric typewriter on a wooden table with castors, set to one side but readily accessible from the velvet chair. At the centre of the table, in a clear crystal vase, stood a single white rose.

To his right the wall was a soldiery of books, marshalled into erect platoons by the immaculate alignment of the shelves. He resisted the temptation to review the troops. In the subdued light, the opposite wall appeared to recede. He could see that the wall paper was soft and delicately patterned and his eyes were drawn to the bamboo framed painting that hung at the centre. Again he suppressed an urge to take a closer look but managed to discern the figures of three children reaching out toward some unseen person or object. Inverting his head backwards he noticed that the wall behind supported a mass of photographs, each in its own frame and positioned with random precision. Responding to the strain in his neck, he brought his head forward and closed his eyes.

From down the hall Paul could hear the last 'good nights' and 'don't forgets' as the child care staff moved through the bedrooms before settling down to the inevitable task of reporting on the observations, encounters and events of the day. So much was familiar to his experience, but there was something else. The questions and doubts that preoccupied him were inescapable evidence of things unfamiliar. In some fundamental way this shift, his first at Willoughby House, stood apart from all that he had come to know as child care work during his two and a half years in the field.

Lifting his feet to rest upon the coffee table where, obviously, many feet had rested before, he struggled to identify the differences but they remained elusive. The kids were more emotionally expressive than he had come to expect but, for the most part, he recognized their behavior as typical of 'troubled' teenagers living in a treatment group home. His three co-workers seemed remarkably at ease with the emotional instability of the group although there was certainly nothing remarkable about their handling of disruptive behaviors. He recalled two or three incidents that screamed out for specific interventions to stem the tide of chaos, but these had been allowed to escalate and dissipate without action. Paul wondered about the kind of training his new colleagues had received. He was unhappy with himself for not moving in but, conscious of his status as a newcomer, he had sat with his frustration, reassuring himself that there would be other opportunities.

He found comfort in his criticism. Whenever he suspended such judgements, however, he was drawn back to the intricate and penetrating texture of the interaction among the staff and the kids. He could touch it only at the very broadest level, as a certain 'energy' that seemed to bring people together, without the imposition of predetermined tasks or the prescriptive framework of specific program designs. For long periods the entire group seemed to be involved in a loosely structured meeting that frequently broke up into smaller encounters without notice. There were times when individual workers would detach themselves with one particular youngster and engage in what was referred to as "personal work." These encounters took place in various parts of the living room and kitchen but, from what Paul could see or hear, they were hardly textbook child care interventions. Sometimes the content and associated feelings from these dialogues were reported back to the group as a whole and a collective analysis would take place. In this process, he was surprised to find that the focus upon the experience of the child care worker was as intense and time-consuming as the focus upon the experience of the youngster. He questioned this and wondered who was in charge and who was in treatment.

He continued to vacillate between question and judgement until disturbed by Charlotte entering her office carrying two mugs of steaming hot chocolate. She placed one on the table in front of him and, settling herself in a chair opposite, proceeded to sip from the other while peering at him over the brim.

She seemed smaller and older than his earlier impression, gained while watching her move quietly and unobtrusively around the perimeter of the evening session. Her participation was never direct but he discovered that he was constantly aware of her presence. At first he attributed this to a familiar sensation of being evaluated but, over the course of the evening, he came to the conclusion that all of the others, kids and staff, were connected to her in some intangible way. He now guessed her age to be somewhere in the early thirties. He judged her to be a woman of considerable determination, assured in her sense of independence and he speculated that she would live alone rather than accept the compromises of a primary relationship. Her presence was powerful but there was a softness that aroused his senses and his curiosity. The dark eyes that engaged him from across the table were steady and sure but, set within the gentle features of her face and framed by the straight black lines of her hair, she offered a strange Oriental serenity that drew him in. 'So you're to be my supervisor,' he thought to himself.

"How are you, Paul?" The question could have been trivial and routine but it was not. Her presence seemed to precede her words and he sensed an invitation to come forward without rehearsing a reply. Caught in the moment, he hesitated.

"It was . . . er, very interesting," he began as he tried to decide how much to share."

"My interest is with *you*, Paul. I'm not too concerned with the 'its' at this point." It was clearly a rebuke but her eyes were smiling and he accepted the clarification with a nod. He continued to wrestle with words that might dissolve the tension between her interest and his confusion.

"I'm curious. I guess that's the best word to use."

"Great, I can't think of a better motive for working with kids, can you?" She waited for him to continue.

"Well, I'm trying to figure out what your program here is all about." He decided to risk. "You're obviously using approaches that get kids in touch with their feelings but what happens then? I can't see what's being done to bring about change . . . where does the treatment come in?"

"Oh dear, you want to know about techniques. I was hoping that you were curious about yourself, about the kids, or even about people in general. Child care is about people, *car* care is about techniques."

"Oh come on! I'm only talking about basic child care methods," he protested, catching his own defensiveness as he listened to the words.

"And what are they?"

"Well for sure, *consistency* is one," he declared, realizing that he was turning defense into attack. "Giving feedback that helps kids to learn appropriate behaviors or support them in building self-esteem. Moving in to prevent kids from sinking too far into their own confusion, anger, depression, hostility or . . ."

"Or their own happiness, joy, serenity, love. . . ."

"No, of course not." He was ready to take a stand.

"Well, what's the difference?"

He was off to a bad start. He tried to reach beyond resentment and recover the principles and beliefs that had served him well. "Those are the feelings that make life worthwhile. They help kids to believe in themselves and encourage them to look to the future with hope. Good child care creates positive experiences. It teaches kids to cope by making them competent. It encourages them to move away from the garbage and go after the good things that life has to offer." It was trite but he meant it.

"So, you've learned that some feelings, actions and experiences are *good* and some are *bad*. You invite children to know and believe only in the positive parts of themselves. You've developed skills that encourage kids to take what you determined to be good and avoid what you determine to be bad. I suppose you measure your success by the willingness of the kids to buy into the package." There was no sign of tension or anger in her voice but Paul continued to do battle.

"No," he stated emphatically. "Success comes when the kid learns to do things well and accept responsibility for his actions. . . ."

"Responsibility comes from a belief in freedom." This time she interrupted decisively with the clear intention of being heard. "That means freedom to explore *all* experience as it occurs. It cannot come from being led toward what others judge to be 'good' and dragged away from what is deemed to be 'bad.' Self-responsibility is not achieved in the context of another person's project; particularly where that project is to coerce the young person into taking pre-determined directions. This is the adult quest for power and control. It's as dangerous for the child care worker as it is for the child."

At this point, Paul considered stepping aside. He knew that his defenses had moved solidly into position and he would sooner or later resort to some form of personal attack. He had not expected things to move this quickly and was sorry he had risen to the issue. He had made a considerable commitment to the professional development of child care and wondered why it was necessary for him to defend this position to someone in the role of a supervisor. He was angry. Charlotte, on the other hand, seemed perfectly comfortable and at ease with the dialogue. Sensing that this gave her the immediate advantage, he tried to dilute the intensity of the discussion. "I'm always willing to learn from others. That's why I left my old position and applied here."

His attempt failed. Charlotte was not about to be lured off course. "You will learn nothing from others," she continued, taking up his point immediately. "Nobody can teach you anything until you come to know that you are already the expert on the subject that lies at the heart of all learning . . . the subject of you. Do you want me to do to you what you were talking about doing to kids? Do you want me to decide what's good and what's bad? Do you want me to reward you for doing things my way, dishing out nice positive feedback when I have you believing and behaving appropriately? Do you want me to ask you to be happy when you're sad, play monopoly when you're angry, or think about the weekend when you're contemplating suicide? Do you want me to re-direct you from all of your own experiences so that you might become competent, well adjusted and accepted?

"If you go along with me in all of these things, abandoning your ability to make choices at every turn, you will learn nothing of yourself and, from here, you will learn nothing about life. You won't even learn anything about me. You'll be selling out to what the experts call 'learning theory' — an absurdly trivial perspective that we have allowed to stand in the way of human development. You will learn nothing at Willoughby House unless your primary interest is in you and your ability to take charge of your life. If your curiosity is here then all of us, kids and staff, can share and contribute, but always with the knowledge that you are the expert on the subject of you. If you're more interested in 'things' that influence, effect or control others, you're in the wrong place."

The lecture came to a stop as abruptly as it had begun. Paul's mind was a mess and he was still angry. He closed his mind to the woman and erased the final vestiges of sensuality that he had been creating between them. With her soft pedantic style, she had established herself as an adversary. She was dismissing him with disdain, challenging him to fight back. She was testing his mettle as a combatant, as a child care worker — as a man. He prepared himself to re-enter.

"We're talking about kids for God's sake. They're not born as philosophers. They're not born as competent adults. They don't come into this world understanding your fancy concepts of freedom and knowledge. They have to learn how to live in this screwed up world and if we don't teach them, then who the hell will? Most of the kids you have around here will be total failures who continue contributing to their own miseries unless we step in and do something about it. That's why I'm in child care . . . not to sit on my fanny and contemplate the nature of the universe." He fell back into the chair with a dramatized sigh of frustration.

Charlotte showed no response to his anger or to the final touch of drama but she reflected upon her own position with a note of sadness. "Even most adults don't see learning as a process of self-exploration based on choices. They struggle to cope. They seem to absorb simply what others tell them and spend their lives hanging onto fragmented bits of information in order to earn a living, maintain a reputation, or protect themselves from each other. They seem to regard themselves as victims of the external world, subjected to the limitations of imagined psychological laws. Even the trivial choices they make are set against some external standard of what is right or wrong, good or bad. How are we ever going to teach kids that life is a powerful force and not a passive pastime. It's a process, not a performance." She paused for a moment allowing her sadness to show and Paul's anger began to dissipate. For some reason, her failure to respond to his gauntlet did not feel like a dismissal. He could actually see her sadness and he wondered about it. Somehow it seemed more real than his anger. She looked across at him and smiled as if to celebrate a moment of contact and, as he felt the tension subside, he began to hear.

"I feel sad when I meet adults who operate this way, Paul, because I assume that, in their own way, they've made their choices and there's little that anyone can do to encourage them to change. On the other hand, like you, I believe that we have a chance, or even an obligation, to encourage young people to take life as an unexplored opportunity. For me the task is one of urging them to examine all that's available through their direct experience with themselves and the world. No, of course they're not born with the skills and the knowledge but these things should be taught or become available in support of their inherent curiosity, as it occurs. Learning should follow the child and not vice-versa. Children need to know as early as possible that they have choices and that their decisions are valuable in the quest for self-discovery and not merely as indicators of competence and acceptability.

"I agree that many of the kids we work with are destined to become tangled up in the world we create but at least our kids have not become so concerned with becoming successful in the eyes of others that they have abandoned their inherent curiosity. What they see may not be highly valued by them but they have no powerful alternative, such as social status, competence or success, to tempt them away. There are still the fears of direct experience and the horrors of self-hatred to be avoided but, with caring, support and acceptance, these can be confronted. Then, if we can look at these things together, what we have to teach becomes useful to the child; not as demands that impose from a controlling world but as information that assists in the natural pursuit of knowledge. If we can achieve this, our kids may not rise to the heights of social status but they will never be prisoners of their own behavior, or puppets for those who wish to demonstrate their power over others.''

"Is this your concern about child care as I was describing it earlier?" Paul's question was genuine.

"Yes, in some respects. If adults have no commitment to self-discovery in its most general sense, they may well become obsessed with their own immediate needs for efficacy or power over others. This can serve the ego by bolstering up the sense of personal autonomy and esteem. Among adults this may certainly support our much adored concepts of competence and achievement. Of course such achievement is shallow and such pursuits run contrary to the project of true self-understanding.

"With adults there's always the possibility that one or other of the competing parties will become tired of the exercise and move on but there are no guarantees. Children, on the other hand, are very vulnerable targets. They are no match for the stronger and more experienced adult and can be trapped into believing that they have little choice, other than meeting the expectations of others. Our kids, thank God, are still fighting, even if only through their own inability to understand what adults expect from them. Oh, they have their own performances but at least these have not become pathologies entrenched through the condescending approval of others.''

Paul was beginning to move with the flow of ideas. "But they do have to learn what adults expect. They need to know what adults will accept and what will be considered unacceptable. The world must speak back to kids as it does to all of us . . . sometimes in words and sometimes in rewards and punishments. To know and predict these things is essential for us to plan our lives as we want them to be. Surely this is the basis of self-determination and responsibility. It comes from experience and, as adults, we do what we can to make sure that kids have these experiences. As I see it the disciplining of a child, by whatever means, is no more and no less than the structuring experience, as a teaching device.''

Charlotte nodded in acknowledgement of Paul's position. "This is why so much rests with the attitudes and intentions of the child care worker and why I was so concerned about your emphasis upon technique. If the worker doesn't make personal learning the primary concern and examine the experiences of the kids from this perspective then I have serious questions about her or his motives. My suspicion is that the primary project will be to make the child into something that meets the workers' own needs for control, acceptance or salvation. This is a selfish reaction rather than a self-full purpose. In the presence of such an adult, no child will be encouraged to examine her own experience or pursue his own unique journey of learning. Instead, the world will indeed speak back, but only from the unacknowledged personal need of the adult to control."

"Sort of a 'my way or the highway' approach to child care, eh?"

"Something like that but without any signs reading 'Highway this way.'"

"But when I work with kids, I know I make moves to control them for my own sake. Maslow might see it as a basic survival need for child care workers. Jeez, none of us are going to walk into a group of acting out kids and let them do whatever. First we have to protect ourselves. Secondly, we have to decide what's acceptable within the particular situation. None of us would keep our jobs if we all had different standards and expectations from those of our supervisors." Paul looked directly into the face of *his* supervisor and winked.

Charlotte wagged her finger in mock chastisement. "The issue is in the overall intent. Of course, I'll control the world around me to ensure my personal sense of safety and well being. Beyond this, I'll test out my efficacy by acting upon my world; this is how I come to understand the incredible potential I have, as well as my own limitations. When I set out to impose myself upon the behavior of a child I may do this in order to protect my own boundaries or my right to pursue my own projects in a responsible way. When I structure a learning situation for a child, as a teacher might set up a classroom, I certainly want the world to speak back to the child.

"These circumstances are quite different in both intention and desired outcome. In the first instance my intention is to preserve my own sense of integrity and I have a very real investment in wanting the child to change. Here the child must come to understand that the issue is one of freedom and not one of control. Developmentally this is a tough one for kids to learn but it's absolutely critical. If this lesson is not learned, control becomes the central theme and children await their turn to exercise it over others . . . it becomes a matter of power rather than freedom.

"In the second case, my attention is focused on the opportunity for the child to learn. Here I cannot invest myself in what the child chooses to do with the information as the world speaks back. Given that I've met my own needs to make sure that the young person is safe from life-threatening danger, my project is one of allowing the child to take the information into her or his own world and examine it in the light of personal experience. Since I can never fully know the private worlds of children, I must assume that they are making decisions that are right for them at that moment in time. These decisions may not be right for me and I may predict that they will not always be right for them but that's what experiential learning is all about. Such decisions are not right or wrong, good or bad, they are just part of learning. Even when decisions made at one time don't fit any more, they can be valued for the time when they did fit and then given up without judgement.

"In child care our task is to be there, available, caring and supporting through this process. Good child care is like a gentle massage from a highly skilled, caring and sensitive masseur. It uses the natural process of growth and development in the same way as the masseur delicately facilitates the movement of energy around the body. It is not the imposition of an outside force created by the wielding of power and authority. When change occurs, it's not the brilliance or tenacity of the child care worker that brings it about — it's a decision on the part of a child who may, in the presence of that worker, decide to take the first risks in the process of self-discovery and self-determination."

"I probably shouldn't ask the question but what's the payoff for the child care worker if it's not some investment in the decisions of the child?"

"A few minutes ago I judged you to be angry. Would this have described your own experience then?"

Paul nodded.

"Somewhere behind the anger was a part of you waiting to be discovered or shared. If you knew that part of you then you could choose to make it available to me and I would learn something about you . . . and thereby something about me. Since your experience was one of anger, I suspect that you don't know that part of you and that your anger kept you distant from the real feeling or experience. In much the same way as we choose not to listen when the world speaks back to us, so we often choose not to listen when we speak back from ourselves. Rather than listen we throw up road blocks, in this case anger. So first, you recognize anger for what it is . . . a smoke screen for avoiding experience and then, you listen. Let me give you an example from child care.

"When you were talking to Crystal this evening she told you many things about herself and, in doing this, she offered you many opportunities for you to look at yourself. Kids, especially these kids, offer us perspectives that are rarely available in the bottled-up everyday world of normalized adult trivia and routine. As they share the rawness of who they are, so we are able to explore and examine ourselves in the raw. They show us the door to our own childhood, and to the child within each of us that has become lost in our struggle to take on the role of adult.

"In your determination to establish and maintain your role as a child care worker by coldly reminding her of the potential consequences for her inappropriate behavior, you probably walked away from a wonderful opportunity to learn something about yourself. It could even be that, like the anger, this decision of yours was a deliberate, even if unconscious, attempt to avoid knowing. Should you continue to do this, you will never explore the realm of self-discovery and you will need other reasons to stay in child care.

"Whatever alternative motives you might have, they will be unacceptable at Willoughby House. Here we look at learning as an exchange. Children learn how it is for adults to struggle in the world as grown ups and we learn more and more about the essential child that will always be part of who we are. Then, together, we learn about ourselves through the sharing of our experiences with one another. This doesn't mean that we don't establish boundaries and expectations for others or, in the case of kids, that we abandon our responsibilities as teaching adults. It merely means that we accept all of these things as personal issues and relate from that perspective.

"That's what's happening right now in the staff room as we talk. I hope that you'll come to experience this . . . as you will if you stay with us. If we were to walk into that room right now, I guarantee that we would not find a group of tired child care workers rushing to get off to the closest bar to unwind. The chances are that we would find a group of people highly energized . . . the type of energy that comes when we truly know that we are discovering something very important. In this case burn out is out . . . that only happens when we're struggling to control while learning very little in the process."

Paul let out another sigh, but this one came from a different place. He was no less confused than he had been at the beginning, but the issues were becoming a little clearer and he wanted time to think. Charlotte seemed to understand his need and made a move to vacate her chair. "I realize that this has been something of a lecture Paul but I wanted to be very clear about our beliefs around here. This is information for you to consider in making your own decisions. From experience I've learned not to beat around the bush on these things. Working here would not be good for everybody. We'll talk again tomorrow Paul; that is if you decide to work at Willoughby House for another day. If you decide not to stay with us, I'd appreciate a call before noon tomorrow as we have a heavy schedule of activities. Meanwhile, at least stay and drink your cold chocolate."

He looked down at the abandoned mug and hesitated. Was she testing him out in some way? If he took the cup would this indicate that he was not making his own decisions? Again she displayed an uncanny ability to understand his dilemma. "Real freedom is choosing to drink your chocolate even if your mother tells you to."

He watched her leave the room.

Looking Professional

Paul returned to the staff suite to retrieve his car keys. The room was in darkness and he stumbled around looking for the switch. He turned on the light to find Geoff sitting motionless at the table. Paul gasped. "Jesus man, you scared the. . . ."

"Yea, I should've let you know I was here but couldn't figure out a way to do it," he explained apologetically. "Marlene turned the light out for a joke and I just left it that way. Just been sittin' here thinking things over. There's a lot of shit coming up for me these days."

After only one shift and an hour with Charlotte, Paul was able to translate the statement into, "I'm looking at some painful issues arising from my personal learning process." With this translation he felt superior. There was something pervasively vulgar about this dissipated, bird-faced little man in the baggy corduroy pants and stained sweatshirt. He was probably no older than Paul but his general demeanour, particularly around the kids, was that of a middle aged ne'er do well with an adolescent fixation. Following the shift, Paul had actually intended to ask Charlotte about him.

He took his keys from the desk and was turning to leave when he grasped an opportunity. "Would you care for a beer Geoff? I'll buy."

Tuesday night and the bar was deserted. Geoff had no formal training in child care. Discharged from the Navy on medical grounds, he took a personal rehabilitation workshop led by Charlotte and became 'hooked.' At his request, she agreed to provide him with a one year 'internship' at Willoughby House. That was eight months ago. "I've got no qualifications for this stuff — nothing to put on my wall but latex." They sat down.

Paul paid for a jug of beer and began to frame his questions. Geoff talked easily. "I've learned a lot at this place. The others tell me that six months of working with Charlotte is worth six years of college but I wouldn't know. I wish I could get a degree at Willoughby House. I don't want to waste my time with school crap at my age but who's going to accept my qualifications? It sure must be nice to be 'legit' though.''

It did feel good to be 'legit.' It was good for Paul and good for the profession. Geoff, on the other hand, was obviously struggling and could only detract from the professional cause. Watching and listening, Paul wondered about Willoughby House. He also wondered about Charlotte. Meanwhile, he drank his beer and asked for more of the story.

Geoff Manning won 'top student' honors in junior high and received a national mathematics prize when he was twelve. He was the protege of his maternal Grandmother, his sole caregiver and guardian from his seventh birthday to his fourteenth year. Before this his life was a hell. He and his younger sister were removed from their parents following a police investigation of the "satanic community" that directed their lives. At Paul's request, he gave graphic accounts of rituals in which he and his sister were forced to perform. While living with his Grandmother, he had no recollection of these events although he persistently experienced terrifying nightmares. Professional help failed to uncover a cause or offer a solution. Meanwhile, his academic achievements continued to elicit the nod of admiration for his Grandmother, his school and the small village where they lived.

When he was thirteen, the logical systems of his brain, that had worked so frantically to mask and contain the turmoil of his mind, finally seized up. Even the most rudimentary steps of elementary arithmetic moved beyond his grasp. Nobody could offer any explanation and he was discreetly transferred to a special residential school conveniently located in a distant community. Only he and his Grandmother knew about the strange marks and indentations that carved themselves into his body each evening leaving no trace the following morning.

At the residential school he was just another boy with a learning problem. In a way, he enjoyed his role as a 'retard.' Free from the expectations of enthusiastic adults and the sneers of green-eyed kids, he rocked himself gently in the frigid corners of cinder block classrooms. He was an oddity and people left him alone. The staff psychologist probed and pestered for a while but eventually gave up. Three abnormal E.E.G. reports suggested a "neurological dysfunction, manifested in early adolescence and probably of unknown genetic origin." There was nothing of interest for the psychologist to explore.

In his sixteenth year, he took-off on three occasions. These were not gestures designed for some anticipated effect upon others. Describing them as "wanderings" and "rambles," he was responding to a permeating discontent, punctuated by recurring images and episodes of insufferable terror. At the most unbearable times, he sold himself for whatever purpose would bring the money for the drugs. Sometimes there would be adventurous or peaceful relief. Then there were the bad trips — the filth, the stench, the police, the hospital and, eventually, the return to school.

When he was sixteen, Grandmother signed the necessary papers and he acceded to their wishes that he join the Naval Cadets. By this time, the pain was in his body. He avoided sleep, anticipating the terror of his dreams and the agony that began through the nausea of the stomach and inevitably transformed into the excruciating cramps and contractions of his bowels. Medical analysis revealed nothing. Finally, the problem was attributed to his heavy drinking and irresponsible lifestyle. He was court marshalled on two occasions for neglecting critical responsibilities.

He was discharged, with a small pension, at the age of twenty-six and went off to find his own niche in the world. His Grandmother was dead and his sister had left no clues. The prospect of looking for his parents was repugnant, although he was never quite sure why. In sullied rooms with wretched acquaintances he tried to find some meaning beyond the pain. He fell in love and confirmed what he had come to suspect and fear — that his body no longer responded to his sexuality. His torment became unbearable.

It was a nurse in the Emergency Department who arranged for him to take the introductory rehabilitation program. A malignant growth in the wall of his stomach was the medical concern, but the nurse saw his despair in the dying embers of his spirit.

The evening class was being led by a psychologist who referred to herself as a child care worker. "We are all dealing with our childhoods," she said. Geoff reflected briefly on the disconnectedness of his life but the moment came and went. Later, when the other students had left and the teacher placed her hand gently on his arm, some connection took place. At the end of the six week course, she agreed to see him on Saturday mornings for private counselling.

In his work with Charlotte, more and more connections began to take place. Beginning with the terrifying images that plagued his mind and, working through the agony that racked his body, the denied horrors of his childhood made their way back into his life. There were times when he would scream in fear or pain. There were times when he would stink—choking on his own vomit with the obscenities that entered his head and violated his mouth. And, in session after session, she stayed with him, hearing, understanding, encouraging and gently holding him as the torment left his body and he allowed his strength and serenity to enter.

Piece by piece the picture began to take shape, each image, event and feeling finding its place within the epic of his life. People, places and experiences, once murky or erased, became decoded like images springing from a television screen with the removal of a scrambler. As all of this was taking place neither he nor Charlotte realized the dangers of having such information.

Geoff was not inclined to make a secret of his 'therapy' or the dramatic nature of the revelations. The threats that he and Charlotte began to receive awakened them both to the far reaching implications of their work together. As a form of protection, Geoff let it be known, through the same channels, that all of the information from the sessions had been fully recorded and placed in a vault. Those with access to the vault had been given instructions to release the documents should anything unusual happen to either of them.

This was not the type of story that Paul had expected to hear but, staring across at his dishevelled colleague, he never doubted its authenticity for a moment. He was overwhelmed by the drama and moved by the humanity of the story teller. He wanted to say something but nothing came forward. He glanced down at the table to find that the jug of beer was almost completely intact. He lifted it in a gesture toward Geoff and filled both glasses. Then something did come forward.

"You are 'legit' Geoff. You have learned what schools can never teach. I'll teach you what I know in the next three months if you'll spend a few years sharing some of your knowledge with me.''

"You've got a deal old buddy. And if you fail I can now go back to school and become a mathematician.''

Paul raised his eyebrows to register his question. ''What about the growth in the guts?''

Geoff nodded. They clinked their glasses together and drank.

Do I Know You?

The decision to stay at Willoughby House, at least for one more shift, had been made without a moment's thought. It was a terrible mistake.

Moping his way down the hallway toward Charlotte's office, Paul was overwhelmed by his own sense of incompetence and angry with himself for his stupidity. How could almost three years of training and experience have evaporated within the span of a few hours? How could he have walked into this charade with eyes wide open after the embarrassment of last night's supervision session with Charlotte? Why had it taken twenty-four hours for the unreal world of Geoff Manning to lose its fascination and reveal its distortion? In his naivete, he had suspended his rationality and his professional aspirations, letting himself in for his worst experience in child care.

Throughout the entire shift his three co-workers had violated most of the basic principles of child care, while ignoring him and his efforts to bring some semblance of order and purpose to the proceedings. His one-to-one time with Michael, a sullen but volatile sixteen-year-old who seemed to set the tone for the entire group, had been bizarre and senseless. Then, to put the final touch on all that was already out of place, his three colleagues declared, and even documented, that the evening had been "exceptionally productive."

By the time he had seated himself in the armchair that had welcomed him so warmly on the previous evening, his deliberations were being cultured in a medium of anger. He concluded that the rejection of him by both staff and kids had been a deliberate ploy to invalidate his professional background and 're-train' him in their own undisciplined ways. Even in this they were incompetent, however, since his sporadic attempts to follow their lead had not even been noticed, let alone reinforced. His fleeting satisfaction reverted

$$\frac{25}{78}$$

back to anger as he recalled their total abandonment of him when his confrontation with Michael almost developed into a major revolt, with most of the other kids siding with their fellow resident.

For Paul this was an unforgivable violation of a principle that lay at the very heart of good practice in group care and treatment. In all the places he had worked, the mutual support among the workers was a sacrosanct and cherished given but, for some misguided reason, these people had shown a total lack of concern for a colleague struggling to find a place for himself in a totally strange environment — so much for caring and sensitivity. For as long as he could remember he had wanted to be part of a group that stood together, nurturing, supporting, encouraging and caring in the face of a cruel and uncaring world. In his chosen profession, he had come to rely upon the mutuality of the team and its ability to create a coherent and consistent environment for the youngsters it was designed to serve. But none of this was to be found here.

Through all of this Charlotte, his supervisor and potential support, had chosen to remain in the background, busying herself with peripheral tasks. Rarely involved, never supporting, she was always watching. He entertained the possibility that she was actually afraid to become involved, in spite of her powerful presentation in supervision sessions. Perhaps she was afraid that her precious concepts and ideas would quickly dissolve in the rough and tumble of a group of bitter, irrational, unresponsive and uncompromising teenagers. Paul reminded himself that he had met a number of self proclaimed experts who steadfastly refused to put their ideas or themselves onto the 'front line.'

Everything about Charlotte was so detached, clean and uncluttered — just like the girls in school who were so self righteous and assured, remaining aloof to ignite his self-doubts and fear of abandonment. How he had watched them from a distance, dreamed about walking them home, strolling through woods, beside rivers, holding hands, speaking softly about feelings, about love. But always, they had turned their pouty mouths and peachy faces toward their worlds of ice cream and velvet lawns, leaving him — sometimes with a snigger — to live with his wretched alley-way and broken finger nails. What he couldn't have, he began to despise.

Charlotte entered the office with mugs of chocolate clasped in each hand. She delicately closed the door behind her with a supple movement of her hips and leaned across the table to place one of the mugs in front of Paul. In this attitude, her face was no more than a few inches from his and he was momentarily enveloped within her physical presence. He resisted the temptation to move back, investing himself in the power drawn from this moment of servitude. He needed to touch his own sensuality and he pushed himself forward, moving his resentments aside to make way. It was an act of courage for him to look at her like this but he was determined that things should change between them.

"How are you Paul?" she asked, taking the chair opposite. She seemed to notice the difference.

"Fine," he lied, taking the mug in both hands and putting it to his lips in the hope of avoiding further deception. Then, in the silence that followed, he slipped back into resentment. He reminded himself of a group therapy instructor who deliberately allowed prolonged silences in order to 'test out' the comfort level of the students. Past resentments combined with present anger to produce a bitter challenge. "Well, here I am. It's time for my evaluation. You have the floor. You have the power—for the moment anyway."

She recoiled visibly from his hostility. Then, focussing her eyes steadily upon him, she drew in a breath and responded. "The evaluation must come from you. It's your experience, not mine, that contains the important information about your work tonight." She appeared self-contained but he noticed a hesitation and sensed a quiver of apprehension. He wanted to push his advantage.

"Oh, come off it! Are you trying to tell me that your opinions are worthless? Surely we're not going to play around again. Supervision is feedback time. It's your turn and I'm waiting." For a moment he thought he sounded silly but he was charged and ready to take her on at all costs.

"My opinions are very important to me Paul and I'm always ready to share them with people who are able to accept them for what they are; but they reveal lots about me and very little about you. They are statements created from my own experience. As such, they are not pronouncements on the way things are. For somebody else they should be no more than interesting perspectives to be considered as they attempt to understand me and the world I create. If I anticipate that the other person is about to take my opinion as definitive statements about *them*, I'm inclined to keep my thoughts to myself. At this moment Paul I have the impression that you're ready to violate what I have to say in this way.''

"My God you're good at getting off the hook around here. I ask for feedback and I get another bloody lecture on philosophy. No wonder the kids are out of control and the staff are totally unpredictable from one moment to the next. It's like walking on another planet.''

Charlotte was clearly shaken by the intensity of Paul's aggression. For a moment he thought he saw tears in her eyes but, struggling with his own turmoil, he was unable to move out far enough to be sure. They sat in a mutually created silence until Charlotte, her eyes still fixed upon his face, opened the door again.

"I could see your pain tonight Paul and your anger comes as no real surprise to me. What we do here is probably quite different from your experience elsewhere and I really do want you to examine what you find at Willoughby House. In this, I'm more than ready to share my personal perspectives with you.''

"Then why are you holding back?'' He sounded sulky and regretted the question. He wanted to be treated like a grown up.

"Because we're talking about *you* and on this subject *you* are the expert. Whatever I have to say about me and my perspectives must be considered in the light of your experience. I want you to examine that experience before considering any thoughts or opinions of mine. If you focus on mine first, to challenge or accept, you'll find yourself struggling in my world instead of exploring your own. If my world and its expectations become more important to you than your own, then you'll spend your time chasing spooks. Ultimately, you'll become tired and perhaps even sick!''

Despite the concern in her voice and the softness in her eyes, Paul sensed that the smugness was returning and feared that his position was being swept toward insignificance once again. He rose to the challenge. "I'm not asking you to evaluate *me*,'' he said with shaky but slow deliberation, "I'm expecting you, as my supervisor, to evaluate my performance.''

"And I refuse to make a distinction,'' she replied softly but firmly. "Other than at the theater I'm not really interested in performances Paul, I leave that to the behaviorists and the competence specialists. For me child care work is essentially the *person*. With performances it is so easy to turn the person into a performer and there is little to be learned in this. I've come across so many child care programs where performance is the key — performers dealing with performers to the point of negligence and abuse. It will never happen here . . . not while I'm around anyway.''

Floundering once more in the unknown and relentless waters of Charlotte's beliefs, he began to panic. Of course he wanted to know what she thought about his work, his skills, his aptitudes. He was prepared even for criticism — as always he had left enough questions about her to dismiss her comments in the service of his ego if necessary. But she had no right to evaluate him as a person. How dare she make assumptions beyond his behavior? Even if she turned out to be right, these were things that could not be changed readily, for her or anybody else. If she could actually see these things, all would be lost anyway. By holding back on her performance-evaluation, she was holding him for ransom — forcing him to grope in the dark for his acceptability.

Struggling with the pain of residual anger and resentment, Paul knew that he would need to remain silent in order to survive. He thought about leaving but the idea was fleeting. He detached himself from Charlotte and went inside — to an analgesic place where there were no thoughts or feelings. Here he knew that he was safe, protected from those around. His mother's voice was a remote and meaningless memory of the world outside.

''Look Paul, I don't want you to close out on me, although I'll respect your decision if that's what you want. I do have opinions and judgements of you and I am prepared to share these if we can establish a clear framework for doing this. I want you to understand what my words mean to me and that they may say nothing that is true about you. I believe that your pain during the shift and our struggle here arise from this basic issue. I truly want to share my thoughts with you and want you to respect my experience. But first, you must trust the integrity of your own. These are the fundamental principles of communication. We have a framework for doing this, if you're interested in pursuing our relationship further.''

As always, he had left one antenna protruding from his place of safety and he allowed her words to filter through. He said nothing but nodded for her to continue.

"This isn't easy stuff to play around with," she challenged. "If you're not fully focussed here with me, we'll just dig a deeper hole for ourselves. I'm not prepared to work on this unless you bring yourself fully present."

He had been given an ultimatum and wondered about the payoff. If it wasn't to be his allowance or a ride in Uncle Marty's car, was it really worth the effort? Maybe she was keeping something back . . . a surprise perhaps. He felt a flash of excitement and opened himself up to the anticipation of a reward. He offered a contrived and familiar apologetic smile. Then he waited.

She paused for a moment, leaning toward him as if to take a closer look. Their eyes connected and his empty smile faded. "Paul, I believe that, whatever is going on inside, you're still interested in what I have to say because you are inherently curious. You may want to hide from information that doesn't fit but that hardly makes you unique. I don't believe that you've already decided to protect yourself behind habitual thoughts and routinized actions."

"Well that's an untested assumption on your part." His observation was spontaneous and without malice.

"I agree, and this leads me to the point I want to make. My picture of you, along with all the assumptions I make, is nothing more and nothing less than *my* picture. If we are to understand one another, I must be able to share my picture with you—help you to see it through my eyes. In order to do this I must take full responsibility for the picture, as an artist might look upon her creation. The more I attribute my picture to you, the more I absolve myself of personal responsibility. If you are to look at *my* picture of you without putting up defensive or ego-based road blocks you must allow me to own it; as you must know and own yours. Once we both accept our responsibility in this, then we need to find ways to communicate our pictures. Let me take a moment to draw an example from what I observed during your shift this evening.

"I want you to think back to your discussion with young Janet just after supper. You walked into the lounge and what first drew your attention—what did you see?"

Paul thought for a moment. He was still caught up in his resentments but saw an opportunity to come out of the cupboard and try again. He cast his mind back to the event. "I saw Janet sitting in the green wicker chair."

"So, from all of the possible stimuli in the room, you were immediately drawn to the young girl in the green wicker chair."

"That's hardly amazing since she was the only person around."

"No, it's not amazing but it *is* interesting. I can think of some people who would be drawn immediately to the light that shone from the kitchen, or the painting on the far wall or the clock above the fireplace. All of these things were within your field of vision but you focused upon the girl in the green chair."

"Is there some kind of mystery here?"

"No . . . just Paul beginning to draw his own pictures by deciding what he wants to attend to at that moment. Had you been late for a meeting, you might have focused upon the clock. Had you been particularly hungry you might have focused upon the light in the kitchen. . . ."

"And had I been interested in junk, I might have focused upon that crappy picture." He was beginning to feel like a student.

"Sure. The first step in taking ownership for the way you create your world is to recognize that you decide where to look. Actually this may occur through any of the senses — smell, sight, sound or E.S.P. The interesting aspect of this is that this decision contains considerable information about you . . . your interests, desires, needs and the like. In fact, you could probably know everything there is to know about yourself by examining where you chose to focus your attention within the space of twenty minutes but that's another story. Right now my point is that no two people begin their pictures by seeing the same thing. Everybody's picture is unique from the very beginning."

"I'll bet most child care workers would focus upon the girl in the green chair."

"That could be, but let's push a little bit further. What did you notice then about the girl in the green chair?"

"Okay. I saw that her head was bowed, one hand was clasped to her forehead and the other was shaking."

"She was also sitting with her legs crossed. One of her socks had a hole in it and her eyes were closed. Now I wonder why you chose to concentrate upon the head and the hands. What was it about them?''

"God, I don't know. She just looked upset . . . she was distressed. That's why I went over to her in the first place."

"So you've already imposed an interpretation on the scene. You have created a young woman in distress. I wonder why?"

"What's this? I know distress when I see it. I've been in this business long enough for that."

"Well looking out from the light in the kitchen, I saw things differently, but let's stay with your scene for a while. How were you when you first walked into the room. How had things been going for you generally."

Paul felt some of his anger return. "I think you already know the answer to that question. I was thoroughly pissed off."

"You were angry?"

"Yes. I'd been ignored by the other staff for most of the evening and working on your own isn't much fun. Not for me anyway."

"So you were feeling alone, unnoticed and irrelevant?"

"Yea, sort of . . . but I was also sure of my own competence. I knew that I would find a way to do some work, my way."

"And there she was, a girl in distress?"

"Are you suggesting that I invented a girl in distress just to do some work?"

"Not necessarily, but let's just go on a stage further. When you walked into the room you chose to focus upon Janet . . . lets call that your *primary perception*. From what you saw, you created a picture of a girl in distress . . . let's call this your *interpretation*. In your opinion, why was Janet in a state of distress?"

"In the first place, she's a hysterical sort of kid at the best of times. Then, it was obvious during supper that she was trying to get Ralph's attention without success. I knew that he was trying to cool things between them. This is not a guess, he told me so himself."

"Right, let's call these things your *judgements*. Now, on the basis of your perceptions, interpretations and judgements, what did you decide to do?"

Charlotte seemed so sure about where this was all heading that Paul became suspicious. He saw a trap somewhere along the path although he was not sure what or where it was. He hesitated in his response.

"It's okay Paul, this isn't a test. Just play along with me for a little while longer."

"Well you saw what I did. Why do you want me to describe it for you?"

"Because we're talking about your experience, not mine. What I saw was that you went and put your arm on her shoulder but I'm not sure what that was about."

"Oh come on. I wanted her to know that I was concerned about her."

"And were you?"

"Yea, sure." He was not very convincing.

"What were your real feelings about Janet at the time Paul?"

"I thought she was being her usual hysterical self, but I was glad that she was around."

"Because you were looking for a purpose and she gave you one?"

"I'll go with that . . . just for the sake of the example, of course." He smiled. Charlotte nodded.

"So . . . just to keep the example alive of course . . . you felt quite negative toward Janet, but your intention was to communicate concern and your motive was to find a reason for being."

"Phew! I'm not sure I want to live with all of this but let's not kill it at this stage. Where do we go from here?"

Charlotte touched him lightly on the hand. "Let me just review the whole scenario for your consideration. I just want to make sure that we are sharing the same picture. You walk into a room feeling lost and looking for an opportunity to be a child care worker again. The girl in the green chair becomes the object of your attention and you interpret her behaviour to be an indication of distress . . . a girl in need. You make some judgements about her and, based upon these, you decide to act in a caring and concerned way. You have made no attempt to check any of this out with the girl in the green chair. If your picture is accurate, and if you have communicated your intention clearly, then we should have two people working harmoniously in a world that they both know and understand. So what happened?"

"She bloody-well hit me." Paul rubbed the side of his cheek to celebrate the memory.

Charlotte began to laugh. She stifled it at first, placing her hand over her mouth. The sound came through her fingers.

Paul saw a familiar snigger and waited for her to turn away. He was prepared for her rejection and ready to discount her evaluation, and her presence. It was time to go and the only real issue was the inevitable problem of retreating without further losses. He rose from the chair and, in an act of courageous confrontation, he faced his adversary.

Charlotte stood up. The smile had faded and her face was serious. She took a step toward him but, hardening his stare, he stood his ground with grim determination. Their eyes locked in combat, he fought to objectify the enemy — refusing to acknowledge the person beyond the object in his sights.

As his eyes narrowed, hers appeared to open. As he drove her out, she seemed to draw him in. The more he rejected, forcing her to join the others, the more she seemed to invite him back. But these were not the loving and caring eyes of mother offering protection from the fear and pain. There was concern, but there was no pity. There was acceptance without benevolence. There was gentleness without weakness. He knew that he was to make the next move and he was aware that, at some profound level, he was making the decision.

When finally he decided, she seemed to know before he did. She smiled — a different kind of smile — and the concern in her face dissolved into light. He returned a respondent smile in his usual dependent way but, this time, his authentic decision maker came forward. The shackles fell away and the laughter came — at first from the head, but then from deep within. Without hesitation she joined him in the moment and he had an urge to reach out toward her. Of course, he resisted. They sat down in unison in their respective chairs and, for a moment or so, they continued to play with the residual laughter. Things were different now.

Finally, Charlotte picked up the pieces. "I'm afraid we may have destroyed the thread of my project completely Paul. Right now I'd really like to explore what went on in this room over the past few minutes but I don't want to leave the other task incomplete. How are you with all this?"

He waved a hand as if to move the moment along and returned to the theme. "I can't leave it here. I'm in the middle of a mystery novel. Let's leave the examination of the hysteria until later. You go back to being supervisor."

"Well, when our story closed, this guy Sir Paul, striving to demonstrate the chivalry of his profession, had built up a picture of a damsel in distress and had rushed to the rescue but, alas, something was amiss and he received a slap in the chops for his efforts." This time the laughter was mutual and instantaneous. "At this point, we know lots about Sir Paul, but the damsel, and her situation, remain a total mystery. Our well intended Knight has responded only to his own view of the world and his own feelings. Lady Janet is no more than a creation of his noble and fertile imagination. He has responded, not to Janet, but to himself. What's more, he seems to have been concerned primarily with his own evaluation of his performance in the role of Knight. In this, he is completely responsible for all of his actions. She, on the other hand, is responsible for the whack in the kisser, but who knows what that was all about? He has refused to take responsibility for his own pictures and actions and is about to blame the whole thing on the damsel. In so doing, he had removed the possibility of the damsel ever becoming responsible for her own experiences and actions."

"Hold it right there. So Lady Janet doesn't exist eh? My supervisor has finally declared her existential position. I'm not sure I want to get into this one. I can feel my head starting to spin already." He held up his hand in protest.

"You don't have to get into anything Paul. But, yes, I am suggesting that the reality of Janet has not impressed itself upon you at this point in our analysis. So far, you have simply responded to yourself but even this information is being lost since you seem to be examining yourself from the position of someone else."

"Eh?"

"It's as if you're evaluating your performance as a child care practitioner from some external frame of reference. Does this make any sense to you?"

"Well, sort of. Of course I worry about what other people expect from me."

"This was my concern earlier when I refused to share my judgements with you. It would be interesting to know whose expectations were in your mind during your interaction with Janet but I'll leave that one with you. At this point I want to point out that the reality that was Janet could only begin to impress itself upon you if you were open to that possibility and took the action necessary to make it happen."

"You mean I should have asked her before moving ahead with my own assumptions."

"Yes, but first you need to be aware of your assumptions and then check them out. This way you take ownership for your picture and demonstrate that you are prepared to modify your perceptions in the light of whatever Janet might have had to say. As it was, you both worked from your own worlds and they turned out to be incompatible. So what happened?"

"Hell, it turned into a shouting match."

"And how did you feel about that?"

"I was angry — bloody angry."

"Angry doesn't count. What was your real feeling?"

"Rejection I suppose."

"Did you feel lonely."

"Hm!"

"Paul, it seems to me that you spent a good deal of your time this evening with resentments that masked your feelings of loneliness and rejection. Based upon your pictures and self evaluations, you withdrew from what was going on without ever stopping to check out your perceptions, judgements, feelings or intentions. In this you missed all of those opportunities to learn important things about you and the others. Furthermore, in my judgement, you took your pictures to be *true* and yourself to be *right*. By definition, this makes the others *untrue* and, therefore, *wrong*. In this way, you absolved yourself of responsibility for the way things were and how you felt about them. This left you free to reject, sulk or whatever."

"Don't be stupid. Only the kids pull that kind of irresponsible stuff. I'm far too mature. Anyway, suppose I was right. Suppose all of my perceptions were accurate and my judgements were appropriate to the experiences of the others. And suppose I really *did* communicate all of these along with my intentions. How would you know?"

"I wouldn't . . . and neither would you, unless you took the time to examine all these things and check them out. Even then, you would still be responsible for your own pictures and whatever you choose to do with them. On the other hand, would you like to know what *really* happened?" She lowered her voice to a whisper and looked from side to side in a gesture of secrecy.

"Be gentle with me," he whispered in return.

"Well our girl Janet was sitting alone in this room, see. She has her transistor radio plugged into her left ear. She's concentrating on the latest cacophany from her favorite rock group, her hand shaking in time with the music."

"Oh, no."

"Oh, yes. And what's more she's not in the best of moods. You see, she's just had a fight with Margaret, the housekeeper, who wanted her to put the radio away and get on with her chores. But now, just as the music is coming to its synapse-shattering climax, in walks this new child care person called Paul. She kinda likes him and checks him out quickly as he enters the room. He looks friendly enough and she goes back to concentrating on her audio delights. Then, as the final bars are making it all happen, she feels a hand on her shoulder. He looks serious and about to take action. He's come to enforce Margaret's call to the chores. Well, no way man. . . ."

Paul was quick to jump in. "You're making all this up. It's pure fantasy to make a point. It can't have been that bad. I'm not that stupid and insensitive."

"There you go with the evaluation again. You don't need a supervisor, you do it all yourself. How do you know that this is fantasy. Would you believe that when you placed that caring hand on her shoulder, you also pulled the earphone that linked her with her ecstasy."

Paul moaned.

Now I See You

The shift schedule, that mighty design for the lives of all residential child and youth care workers, left him without summons for the following day. He was pleased to have the time for personal reflection, although he had made arrangements to keep his supervision time with Charlotte in the evening. As he collected his clothing for the weekly ceremonial wash, he pondered upon the recognition that he was still employed at Willoughby House.

Mrs. Harrington, a large matronly woman with tightly permed grey hair and large watery blue eyes, was already folding her washing on the table by the time Paul arrived at the basement laundry. She lived with her daughter in 204 and was an active member of the resident's committee. She greeted him with an enthusiastic smile and threw in a full-mouthed "Good morning" for extra measure. He felt intruded upon and made a decision to return to his apartment immediately after setting the washing machine in motion.

"You weren't at the meeting on Wednesday." Her stentorophonic voice casually cast aside the competition from two industrial dryers and a furnace that could be heard from the ninth floor. For Paul, Mrs. Harrington offered three reasons for her affiliation with the human condition. There was her daughter's career as a 'fashion model'—although he suspected that this was a euphemism and occasionally scanned questionable magazines for the evidence. Then, there was her status as the social coordinator for the tormenting resident's committee that gave her a reason to intrude into all lives. Finally, and above all, there was her determination to liberate him from his isolation and loneliness by drawing him toward the meager bosom of her posturing daughter.

As he transferred his clothes from the plastic basket to the waiting machine he knew that her eyes were upon him and he caught himself concealing his undershorts in the folds of other garments. Why did she always do this to him? Why did she have to pry into his life at all? Obviously she lived vicariously through the vulnerability of her victims. Clearly she wanted to claim him as a member of the cast in the trivial drama that she pretended to direct around Westfield Apartments. He was tired of the cat and mouse stuff. He inserted the two quarters, pushed in the slides, waited for the first flow of water and turned to leave. Sure enough, there she was, the moon of her face beaming from the corner. He gave a perfunctory nod and walked toward the door but, on this occasion, the tension within him did not dissolve with the increased distance between them. Again he saw her face and experienced a wave of sadness. "D'ya have time for a coffee Mrs. Harrington?" he asked.

Sitting in Arthur's Coffee Shop, within the abounding presence of Mona Harrington, Paul struggled to share his pictures. Like a student driver with his body in the car and his mind in the manual, he picked his way clumsily through the mechanics of *perceptions, interpretations, judgements, feelings* and *intentions*. He felt awkward, inappropriate and, at times, insensitive but he pressed on, trying hard not to read too much into the facial and bodily responses of his quarry—such perceptions would send him off onto another set of interpretations, feelings and judgements.

She was not pleased with what he had to say. In fact, she was demonstrably upset and angry but he managed to calm her down with disguised apologies and a few liberal spoonfuls of sugar for the medicine that he had clumsily administered. At this point he found himself evaluating his performance and tempted himself just to let her go, but his curiosity had been aroused. Obviously some of what he had to say had been affirmed but 'Happy Harrington' had given some new information about herself—some of it in her anger. It was hard for him to accept that he was actually *interested* in the woman but he really *did* want to know what she had to say. Casting his own stuff aside, he suddenly felt free to listen. Having liberated himself from his own conspiracy of silence, he was no longer her victim. He was in charge, without fear and strangely curious about the world of this wide eyed woman.

Beyond her anger, she seemed to understand that his intentions were not to hurt and that his curiosity was sincere. She agreed to stay and he ordered two more cups of coffee. They talked for well over an hour, oblivious to the unfinished tasks that awaited them in the basement laundry.

When the elevator doors opened at the second floor, Mona whispered a gentle "goodbye" and turned toward Suite 204. In the ultimate world of Paul's experience, she was transformed. The predator had become a person.

Later that day he transformed Elaine Morrison. During a long walk in Sefton Park he cast aside her identity as a sex object, to be pursued through postures of 'masculinity,' and discovered a frightened kid who wanted to be a writer. Without the usual slime of deception and deceit, he shared his judgements and acknowledged his attraction. He also made it clear that it was not his intention to act upon his attraction by pursuing a physical relationship. Divested of hidden agenda and free of his self-doubts in the pursuit, he gently explored the world of Elaine Morrison. Through the insights that arose, he once again looked at the girls at school, at Charlotte, and began to understand himself.

Charlotte laughed without restraint. Paul's comic reconstruction of Mona Harrington's reaction to his judgements reflected the freedom and spontaneity of the day. In his mimicry he was unrehearsed, present, and alive. At that moment, taking on the role of another, he was truly himself. Charlotte knew and celebrated with her laughter.

When the performance was over they were able to look at each other. "Thank you Paul. You are the actor and actor is you. I *see* that you are full of energy and *interpret* this to mean that you feel light in spirit. I *judge* that you have experienced some freedom from your work today and I *feel* a real sense of joy right now. It is my *intention* to encourage you to continue working in this direction!"

Having taken the teachable moment, she sat back in her chair and looked out at him. He went inside. 'I see that you're a beautiful woman, perhaps the most beautiful I've ever encountered. I see that you're looking at me and I interpret that look to mean that you really like me. I judge that you are seeking a special relationship at this point in your life and I feel scared and inadequate because your expectations would be far too high for me. It's my intention to do nothing about it. In fact it's my intention to tell you nothing of what

I'm thinking right now.' He knew that he was cheating and attempted to justify it as practice. Then he looked away.

"You did great work today, Paul. Did you think of it as work?"

"No, not really!" Something had changed between them. He was back in his place as a supervisee and she was sounding pedantic. On the other hand, he was learning and he was happy to stay with the flow.

"I'd like to move this exercise one step further. Are you okay with that?" she asked.

"Sure, although I'm probably working at my limits already."

"Well let's start with some fine tuning . . . like asking permission. You and I have made some agreement to work on these things together but Mona Harrington didn't. Asking a person, including a child, if she or he is interested in your judgements is a simple gesture of respect. Secondly, it's absolutely essential that you take the time to check out your interpretations and judgements with the other person. What they have to say may invite you to reconsider or modify your pictures. This may well be the most critical part of the communication game. Thirdly, it's important for the person to understand that such judgements continue to reflect you and your experience, not them and theirs."

"I still have trouble with this one. It's simple, it makes sense but somehow it's unbelievable. I get tangled up with sympathy, empathy and all that stuff. If all I have is my own experience to work with, then I can never get to know another person at all — especially a kid whose age and experience are totally different from my own."

"I agree with that."

"Agreeing with me doesn't help me to understand what I just said . . . or what you think I just said . . . or what I think you think you just said . . . or. . . ."

"Okay, let me explain it this way. The idea is that when we experience another person, particularly at a feeling or emotional level, we actually experience ourselves. When I cry in a movie theater, as I usually do, I'm not crying for the symbol on the screen or even for the character being portrayed. I'm crying for what that actor represents in *my* own life; my response is to my story and not theirs. Similarly, you must have noticed how child care workers have different responses to the same child. In our business, the story of one youngster may trigger anger in one worker, sympathy in another, alienation in another, despair in another and so on. The child and the story still remain the same, it's the lives of the workers that are different. They respond to experiences that are etched into their view of who they are in the world. Are you with me?''

"I'm not sure. I can see how this would be the case if there was no chance to interact or communicate with the other person. All this stuff we've been dealing with, like sharing and checking out, seems to change all of that.''

"It certainly helps us to reach agreements, but we can never say that we truly know or understand what the other person has experienced. The experience is all our own and it's embedded in a context that is totally unique — the context of our entire life up to that moment.''

"So I spent the day making agreements with Mona and Elaine. That's it? That's all there is? What if they lied?''

"Yes Paul, that's all there is. A truthful person may decide to share from personal experience and a curious person may decide to listen from a place of personal experience. There can be no commonly held *truth* even if they both agree to agree. In this there is no right or wrong, no good or bad — there just is. For two people to communicate, the basic commitment is to use commonly held words and meanings to disclose experience. That's all. If one sets out to deceive the other by distorting personal experience, it certainly throws a wrench into the communication machine. On the other hand, such distortions still provide fascinating information for the person who thinks he is deceiving and the person who believes she's being deceived.

"Even this idea of deception is experiential rather than actual. Here the interest is in the *in*tent rather than the *con*tent. Beyond this is the issue of disclosure. Is the withholding of information a lie . . . a deception? Again we're talking about intent. Given that we rarely know the full extent of our own experience and we can never come to *know* the experience of another person, it seems counterproductive to become enmeshed in the rights and wrongs of it all. In the end, we are still left with our own interpretations, judgements and intentions, and these provide the foundation for the choices that we make. This is where all learning begins and ends.''

"I can see how this might be very freeing. I got myself bogged down with Mrs. Harrington on the 'who's right?' stuff and I'm constantly battling kids on the 'good—bad' nonsense. Then I invest a lot of time in lie detecting, sometimes turning this into a 'right—wrong.' All these things seem justifiable at the time but they sure clog up the communication tube. It's all very interesting."

"From this perspective there are no '*its*,' Paul. You would need to say '*I*' am interested."

"You're right, I am interested."

"No, I'm not right. It's just that you agree."

"Oh God!" Paul sank back in his chair with a sigh and a smile. The naive sense of freedom and curiosity arising from the challenges of the day had become lost in his head. Why did she always do this to him? Jumping from the simple to the complex and back again was tearing his own experience to shreds.

"What's going on Paul? You look perplexed."

"I think its time for a review of the material. I'll never pass the exam at this rate. We are still talking child care aren't we?"

"I believe that we're talking about the very heart of child care. I'm suggesting that parents and child care workers can never really know the kids they work with. However superior we might feel as adults, we can never 'know best.' Since we cannot know the child's own experience, we can never take responsibility for it. The more we try to take this responsibility away from youngsters, the less likely they are to examine and exercise choices of their own. All parents and practitioners would do well to think very carefully about this one. Our experience of the child is within us—our view of what it is to be a kid—and not in the world out there or in that kid's own experience."

Paul held up his hand. "So we can never really know what's in the best interest of a child. We can only guess from our own experience, reflected from what we *think* the child has told us. Is that it?"

"I believe so. We can use our own judgements to protect, nurture, teach or encourage a child. It is also possible for us to have a child respond directly to our judgements and invalidate his or her own experience. Developmentally though, the task is to encourage kids to examine and respond to their own experience. This is what responsibility is all about."

Again, Paul was thoughtful. "I'm still not sure how we superimpose ourselves on kids like this. Most of us were trained to listen and understand. That's what our profession is all about. The kids and the issues are real and our task is to move beyond subjective assessments to something more . . . well, substantial."

"Look, if I see a man coming down the street wearing a clerical collar and he speaks to me with tight-lipped precision, I make all kinds of judgements from my own experience. I'm reminded of times with my father, my English teacher and Aunt Maude. I feel shame around my early experiences of sexuality and I trash myself for stealing that doll from one of my classmates. I dislike this innocent cleric for his tight tongued pretense, his air of superiority and, in my fear, I move away from him as quickly as possible. Having made my move, I then begin to feel guilty because somewhere along the line, I've developed a belief that I should accept men of the cloth." She looked heavenward and continued.

"By the same, token, I've made many negative judgements of kids. Rather than examine myself in all of this, I've held a view that what I experience is real. Here again, I operate from a belief that it is wrong to dislike a child. So I stuff my feelings and make the judgements 'objective.' Sometimes it helps to label a child as 'hyperactive,' 'delinquent' or the like. In our business, our colleagues have provided us with a whole process of assessment and a multitude of labels to help us in dealing with a child whom we might find objectionable. In this way we deny our feelings and justify not sharing them with others. Here we depersonalize the whole judging process and resort to non-sensical statements like, 'sure I care for the kid, it's the anorexia I can't stand,' or 'I love my kid but she's not really responsible for what she does at her age.'"

"I hope you're not trying to tell me that the problem is always with the adult and never with the kid."

"No. Accepting the reality of restricted information and developmental limitations, the youngster is always responsible for what she or he does. I'm suggesting that the adult is always responsible for her or his own judgements and for any actions taken, based upon these judgements."

"But these judgements are based upon what the kid does."

"Well, I believe that they're based in the adult. So, a given kid or a given behaviour will produce very different interpretations, judgements, feelings and responses from different adults."

"So you don't believe that a good assessment or psychiatric diagnosis will add some objectivity to it all?"

"These things may help professionals to agree upon particular judgements and provide parents with an objectifying explanation. As a psychologist, if I happen to share Freud's beliefs I will accept the judgements that arise from a projective test. If I was trained to accept the premises of behaviorism, I might readily accept the conclusions drawn from a behavior rating scale. If, like some of our colleagues, I believe that I am the product of my environment and genetic pre-disposition, then the whole thing becomes pointless since even the judgements that I make are pre-ordained. As for the objectivity of psychiatric diagnoses, I would draw your attention to the research in this area. It is clear to me that, in spite of the attempts of our white-coated friends to create trivial categories for human beings, they can never agree upon who should go in what category.

"The real tragedy is that all of these attempts to create objective labels takes us further from our own direct experience and decreases the opportunities for us to share experiences with others. In other words, it destroys the kind of communication that we've been talking about. Can you imagine it? . . . I *see* that you have a fried egg on your left ear . . . I *interpret* this to mean that you might be different from the rest of us . . . I *judge* you to be a psycho-pathogenic Wombat . . . I *feel* very professional when I use this term. . . . it is my *intention* to go and find some more psycho-pathogenic wombats?"

For some reason Paul felt personally invalidated. He didn't want her to leave him but he wanted to be treated like a grown up, like a professional. "Are you suggesting that it's unfair to lay these judgements—I still prefer to call them assessments—on kids or other people?"

"No. I'm not concerned with fairness. This is a personal assessment belonging to the judgemental framework known as morality. My concern is that we lose so much information about ourselves when we fail to recognize our views as *us*. When we see them as real properties of the real world we focus our attention outwards. Then we find ourselves looking out on a world that determines our destinies instead of creating our destinies from the strength that lies within us. We end up relating to people as objects in a world of objects and deny our very humanity. We become personally irresponsible. Is this what we want for ourselves and our kids?''

"It's easy to take pot shots at adults and professionals from the safety of your office or the privilege of your position." He wanted her to recognize his opinion although he knew that he had yet to put one forward.

Charlotte rose from her chair and adjusted her skirt. She walked toward the bookshelves. "Do you enjoy spending time with me Paul?" The question came as she reached for a volume on one of the lower shelves. He was playing in his head and watching her body. Now she wanted to be personal. This was another ploy of hers designed to throw him off guard. He struggled with honesty but there was too much at stake. He just wanted to survive.

"Sometimes." He waited for her next move.

"Sometimes you do and sometimes you don't?" She came back to her chair, placed a book on the table and sat down.

"Yes, something like that."

"And what, or who, accounts for the difference?"

"Well, I like it when you talk about child care but I don't like it when you go off on bizarre philosophical tangents."

"So I'm in charge eh? What I choose to talk about determines your experience. Do you enjoy turning yourself into my victim? Is that better than taking responsibility, or deciding to enjoy life as a learning experience? Why don't you choose to enjoy being with me no matter what I'm up to?" She moved forward in a gesture of challenge.

He came forward to meet her. "Because you. . . ."

". . . because *I* nothing. All my questions were about you and you throw them straight back to me." She was no longer the serene Oriental princess. She was poised for confrontation. This was not the Charlotte of his experience. The target had changed and his attack became unfocused and confused. He felt naked and exposed. He wanted to cry.

"I think I should leave," he pouted.

"Well a decision to escape would at least be a decision." She was unrelenting and rude.

"So now it's time for insults." His courage began to return.

"Well if you're going to sit there, here's another piece of philosophy for you to feel put down or confused about. I *see* that you are upset and I *interpret* this to mean that you are feeling put down and attacked. My *judgement* is that you are holding me responsible for all of this. How am I doing so far? I'm checking in with you."

"Pretty close. Go on." His lips were tight.

"Oh, I will. My feeling is one of fear and I am turning this into anger. My experience is one of being objectified — placed in a role by you. I realize that only I can do this and this tells you a lot about me. When I find myself in the role of mother I want to run. I want to run away from you but, at this stage, that's not my intention. I want you to understand this Paul. I will not place myself in a position of assuming responsibility for your life or your experience although, as you can probably see, the temptation is there . . . boy is it ever. Sometime, if you're interested, I'll tell you where this temptation comes from but please hear my fear in the moment.

"In a world of victims, villains and saviours, each depends upon the other for validation and esteem. I've always been a saviour looking for victims to save and villains to blame. In some ways I make myself a victim of the system that creates these three absurd characters. In this charade, my life is as hopeless as the others. So, when I see you sitting there feeling sorry for yourself or otherwise victimized, my tendency is to run in and save you — just like I use to run in and save kids when I started out in this business. This was really easy when I saw myself as the villain. My saving was for me, not for the kid but, by turning the kid into a victim-object, I took away her freedom. I paid the price of taking on this responsibility. So, I will not take responsibility for your thoughts, feelings or behavior. You know as well as I do that you are free to stand up and leave. I'd like to tell you how I'd feel about that, but my judgement is that you would suspect my motives . . . you would take something upon yourself that is not yours to take."

This was no philosophical statement. It was Charlotte speaking about Charlotte and he was able to detach himself and listen. At first he felt apologetic and wanted to admit his guilt. In a moment of insight, he realized that this would assault the integrity of her experience and his fear dissolved into curiosity—the same challenge that had taken him into the personal lives of Mona and Elaine. But this was Charlotte, this was different. Again it was clear to him that the communication sequence was the key that disentangled his experience from that of the other person. Somewhere in this trite little ritual lay the seeds of freedom and personal responsibility, but he couldn't quite figure out how this went. With Charlotte sitting opposite, there was no time to think it through. All he knew was that he had become free to listen and understand. Charlotte had been talking about Charlotte and he could think of nothing more fascinating. He sat for a moment before responding.

"Thanks Charlotte. You just taught me . . . sorry, I've just learned something but I can't put it into words yet."

"I want you to try." There was an appeal, an urgency, in her voice.

"Oh dear. Well it's something to do with personal responsibility. My world is full of expectations that I will take responsibility for someone else and this gives me every justification for not taking responsibility for my own experience and actions. I know that this is part of the kid-caring piece but it's also much greater than that. My insight is that the more I take responsibility for another, the more I move away from my own responsibility and the more I encourage the other person—kid or adult—to move away from theirs. This is a sobering thought for me as a child care worker. I'm overwhelmed by how much we foster dependency and how this works against us. Am I making any sense?"

"Well I can link what you say with thoughts of my own, if that's what you mean. The communication exercise we use here promotes ownership. It allows for personal experience to be acknowledged, shared and fully owned by the person. This allows the other to listen without getting entangled in rights or wrongs, goods or bads. Have you noticed any change in our interaction?"

"I judge you to be teaching at this point Charlotte, but yes I have. The tension is missing."

"Of course I'm teaching, Mr. Child Care, but I'm now Charlotte the teacher, not Charlotte playing teacher. Can you see me Paul?"

She cupped her hands around her eyes looking at him through imaginary binoculars.

"I'm not sure but I can certainly see me. Hell, I've really imposed my experience on kids. I've protected myself behind the assessment game, I've got myself in power struggles by tangling my experience with the kid's and I've even taken responsibility for what children choose to do."

"Interesting Paul. Why do you think you've chosen to be just like the rest of us?"

"For many reasons."

"Name some you scoundrel."

"Fear of hurting feelings, for one. I don't like to hurt people."

"Even though you know that this is impossible."

"It is?"

"Of course it is. Think about it Paul. If your judgements belong to you, then the other person has to take them and turn them in on themselves. Even if you intend to hurt them, you can only offer a dagger with the hope that they will then proceed to stab themselves with it. Knowing that a person is likely to attack themselves with your words may influence you to hold back but this is the issue of sensitivity. The primary concern is still one of intent."

"So I'm free to say whatever I like to anybody . . . come on Charlotte."

"Of course you are, as long as you continue to hold yourself responsible for your judgements, your intentions, and your actions. But, please, give the responsibility of the response to the responder. Now, what else holds you back?"

"With kids I worry about their ability to really understand what I say."

"A very real concern. A good parent or practitioner will understand what each child is capable of comprehending. Next."

"It doesn't seem very professional. Oh God, that sounds awful."

"How honest of you. This type of personal communication is certainly a far cry from the abstractions, intrigues and complexities of objective analysis and pretentious psychotherapy but that's why we're in child care. Next."

"I'm scared."

In the quick-fire barrage of question and answer, she had . . . no *he* had . . . put a hole in his defenses. Too late to retreat, he was out there. There was the inevitable silence of fear before the kill.

She leaned forward. "Yes Paul, I think I know. I think I understand. A few minutes ago, you called me by my name for the first time. I felt like a person with you. When you're open and personal with me I feel connected but free." She held out her hand across the table and he took it gently, more as an act of compliance than a desire to touch. He felt the warmth of a blush upon his face. Everything was so out of place . . . potentially out of control. Holding hands with Marjory Cook in the classroom, with his mother at Uncle Marty's wedding . . . the boys laughing, mother smiling behind her protective veil. Here was Paul, poised for retreat, calling upon all of his resources to find a way to keep his image alive.

"Vulnerability can be a very scary place, Paul." Their hands disconnected and he wondered who had made the decision. What was she up to now? Had all of this been planned in order to make yet another point? She seemed sincere yet composed. There was nothing seductive about her manner and yet. . . . "What are you feeling Paul?"

"I'm feeling embarrassed." He managed to look her in the eye.

"Can I call this a feeling of self-consciousness?"

He nodded.

"Good! This is the vulnerability that lies at the heart of learning and growth, Paul. If you can come to terms with your fear, I believe that the questions you have and the answers that you come up with are the real stuff of self discovery. Right now, your questions about me might be the clues to the answers about you, but now I'm being really presumptuous. Thank you for allowing yourself to be seen in your self-consciousness. Your self became present for me too and I like that."

"Are you kidding. I'm not allowing it, I'm fighting to control it. I'm not showing it, just glowing it."

"Oh I'm sure you'll have your armour back on in a minute but what has been shared will always be there. Just as it would be if you took the risk to really reveal yourself to a child. Naturally, you would use discretion and be careful to protect your own boundaries but, responsibly enacted, such sharing between an adult and a child is magic. Let me talk about this for a minute.

"In my opinion, personal vulnerability is the most potent state for all learning. Sometimes we experience this vulnerability as discomfort and give it labels like embarrassment or shame. Sometimes we experience it as joy or sadness and hide it as inappropriate. We fear the judgements that others might make and we run back behind our disguises. But laughing, crying and blushing, tell us and others that we exist. They are the pure essence of our experience — the place where learning begins and ends. Rather than explore these things and allow others to share in our experience we run away and hide. In young babies we see the rawness of these things, finding them in ourselves and taking pleasure. We watch them make mistakes without shame. Babies offer an openness that we lose as we, and they, grow up.

"Eventually we decide that children must learn to control themselves. In taking on the role of teacher, we may launch an assault upon the spirit — the energy of learning. We struggle to meet our needs through the children we teach, evaluating *our* successes along the way. We encourage them to study the meaningless trivia of our agendas and suppress their own curiosity through the punishment and deprivation of bureaucratic school systems."

Charlotte paused and shook her head. "Learning doesn't have to be the blind leading the blind Paul. Somewhere in the direct encounter between ourselves and the world out there lies something called the truth — the truth about who we are and about our place in the scheme of things. This truth can only be found in our experience, but the search can be fueled and enriched by what others have to say about their experience and what our teachers have to say about the world as 'known.'" She wiggled her fingers to symbolize the inverted commas and continued. "So when you question relationships I want to suggest that, the more others share their real experiences with us, the more we are encouraged to examine our own. The information they provide helps us to piece together this gigantic jigsaw that is our lives. Relationships place us at the front end of our direct encounter with ubiquitous truth and, while we can never say that we know another person's experience, what they have to share helps us to know our own.

"I want you to see what I'm getting at here Paul. I'm suggesting that, without the direct examination of personal experience that is made possible through relationships, there can be no search for truth. All we can do is amass, interpret, and categorize information to construct a picture that conforms to some set of arbitrary rules. So, a teacher who gives out such information to children in a classroom without providing the conditions for an examination of subjective experience is an impediment to the cause of learning. By the same token, a child care worker who invites a youngster to accept certain beliefs or values, learn particular skills, or assume particular responsibilities without reference to experience, also commits the same detrimental act. Does any of this fit for you?''

''It does indeed.'' He was now moving with his own experience. ''I was just thinking of the moments when a youngster has opened up in this way. What a privilege and what a learning opportunity. Why would we want to stay apart and deal with children as objects? Kids are supposed to need adults and, from what you say, we have much to learn from the kids.''

''It's too risky. Kids, particularly our kids, have many reasons for protecting themselves. Many don't want to be seen because they're ashamed of what others might find. Some have found sharing to be a very painful or unpleasant experience and have come to mistrust the intentions of others. Then there are those who believe that they have very little to share because they have never been encouraged to look at themselves, or they have been actively encouraged to look away. These are the dependent ones.

''As for ourselves, we seem to be threatened by children for a variety of reasons. We want to show ourselves to be in control and competent. We may be threatened by the child that is in each of us. We may fear the responsibilities that come with parenting, teaching or child caring. For many reasons, we seem to have a powerful investment in the adult role as a vehicle for detachment. Perhaps we don't want to be fully present in case *we* are seen.''

''What about child care workers? Surely *we* have good reasons for looking at ourselves and being present for kids. . . .'' Paul stopped in the middle of his sentence. The memory of his first session with Charlotte flooded into his mind—not so much in words and sentences as in the realization that he had just reversed his position on something profound. The anxiety was instantaneous. 'So this is cognitive dissonance,' he thought, remembering an old psychology class. At first it was like walking into a trap and he was ready to blame someone. He then realized that he was the one looking — that nobody had set up a snare and that he had been doing all the work. He looked across at Charlotte who seemed to be waiting for him to sort it out. "You know what I'm thinking don't you?" he asked.

"No, all I can do is make a guess. I guess you're beginning to understand my concerns about power and control but I'll never know for sure." He nodded back at her and they allowed a comfortable silence to extend between them.

Paul went inside himself with some apprehension about what he might find. He was not concerned with his performance, assured that Charlotte would understand his need for reflection. At a future time, he would come to recognize this moment as one of considerable significance but here, suspended in silence, he allowed his thoughts to drift without direction. He was creating images of his brother Richie when Charlotte's voice did finally intrude.

"Can you recall any moments from your own childhood when you just knew that an adult was fully there for you, fully present? Did you ever experience the vulnerability of an adult?"

Paul fell into silence.

"You look sad Paul. What are you thinking about?"

"I had a school teacher once — his name was Perkins. He never cried or came unglued or anything like that but he was there for me. He was always the teacher but I knew about him, the person. He wasn't full of rah! rah! stuff but he smiled when I did well and was concerned when I struggled. With him I knew that I existed, not as a student, but as a kid. Relatively, speaking I spent very little time directly in his company but he was probably the most influential adult in my life — next to my mother of course. I believe he died alone."

"Isn't that interesting Paul. Somehow, he allowed himself to be seen and you felt validated. If he had cried or come unglued, you might have had a hard time staying with him but that's not what vulnerability is about. These are the dramatic moments and adults may choose not to share them with young children. On the other hand, he did communicate his feelings to you and allowed himself to become present as a person and a teacher. Because of this, those moments you spent together were so special and have stayed with you all of your life. This was not because of his teaching skills, although these might have enriched the encounter. Your Mr. Perkins allowed himself to become a person — to be there — and encouraged you to do the same. Perhaps he died alone but he may not have died lonely.''

"I haven't thought about him for a long time but he's always around in my life somewhere . . . how strange.

"I don't find it strange. In my experience — which is all I have — there are very few people in our lives who just let themselves be fully there without hooks or expectations. This is probably the greatest gift you can give to yourself or another human being. That's why I don't believe that we should throw it about without consideration. As you have already indicated there *is* a risk involved and the fear can be very real. On the other hand, this little communication exercise we're playing with constantly keeps the door unlocked and you are always in the driver's seat. I can appreciate that you might hold back out of fear but, in time, you will see that it actually increases your choices and never leaves you defenseless — unless of course that's how you want to be. At that point, I would recommend the safety of a primary relationship or a group set up for that very purpose.''

Paul was still thinking about his old teacher and putting this experience into his own work with kids. He was beginning to understand what he really had to offer and what the payoff might be. He was about to make some announcement to this effect when Charlotte broke the silence.

"Enough for me, Paul. Before we leave it for the night, I want to introduce the little ritual that we encourage after every shift and encounter around here. This communication design is the basis of what we call 'clearing.' In the interest of staying open to future learning, it's important that we don't carry baggage around that can contaminate the next encounter. So, if we have any unfinished business by way of perceptions, interpretations, judgements, feelings or intentions still hanging around, let's get them on the table and check them out before moving on. When time is short, as it is now, we might restrict ourselves to the sharing of 'appreciations' and 'resentments.' This deals with the major issues that could create problems or blockages. Would you like me to start?''

''Yep!'' He wanted the rules to be spelled out and the method demonstrated.

''On the resentment side, I still judge that you want me to be the authority that confirms your dependency needs and, ultimately, your irresponsibility. Now I want to know that you understand the resentment and that it is my experience and not a part of you.''

He was surprised at the clarity of the statement and it did make sense to him. But suddenly the link between them was no longer ''nice'' and his stomach reacted. ''Yes, I understand what you just said and I accept is as your experience. Do you want me to defend myself?''

''If you accept it as my experience, no defence is necessary. It's information that you now have about me. There's a danger at this point that we could move to a 'yes it is . . . no it isn't' interlude and this would be pointless. Beyond this, if you want to make a comment or observation, that's okay but remember, this is for me. Your turn next.

On the appreciation side Paul, I believe that you are really struggling with many fundamental issues. I appreciate your willingness to stay in there. I appreciate your respect for me, and my feelings, even though we both know that I am the sole creator and guardian of these. I do enjoy my time with you Paul.''

''Thank you.''

''There's no place for thanks here Paul. You are in no position to thank me for my experience. Expressing a positive is not a reward, it's a personal statement made for my benefit.''

''Charlotte — I was thanking you for taking the time to share these things with me. That's all.''

''Whoops. The student becomes the teacher. I stand corrected. Your turn Sir.''

He looked across at this unbelievable woman. There was so much he could say. In her presence his whole life was being called into question and it seemed to him that he spent every moment shooting judgements and feelings in her direction. He picked his way carefully through the possibilities, identifying many of them as inappropriate or bizarre. He decided to play the game but play it safe. He was confident that there would be many other opportunities.

What Is There to Learn?

"Three evenings in a row doing individual work with Keith Potts. It's too much. The kid drives me nuts. I don't care how unprofessional it sounds, I just don't like Keith; in fact I can't stand the guy and I see no point in going on like this." Paul had never made such an appeal to a supervisor before but, at this point, he wanted Charlotte to use her authority to change the assignments. He had agreed to work with Keith for the full week, dealing with particular issues, but something had to be done to preserve his own sanity. There was desperation in his voice that penetrated through his efforts to present an air of professional calm.

Charlotte closed the book that lay open on the desk in front of her and moved to the other side of her office where Paul had collapsed in the most comfortable chair, a leg straddled across one of the arms. She moved over to the coffee table and perched herself on the edge. Her presence filled the space around them. It was calm, balanced and confident. Paul was immediately aware of the contrast between them and clumsily readjusted his own position in the chair. He was still in awe of her in spite of the many hours that they had spent together in this room and in spite of her persistent refusal to accept the authoritarian mantle of her role.

Her response was immediate. "You don't have to work with Keith. Now, what can't you stand about him?" As always, the question probed well beyond the words. It was as if her entire being was totally engaged in this moment of curiosity and Paul was never really sure if her interest was directed toward him, his experience, or some transcendental issue beyond his grasp. He had learned enough to know that a sloppy, poorly articulated response would not divert her from the quest.

"He's a wimp . . . a real wimp. He goes on and on about his mother's rejection of him and wails and moans about his deprivation, whatever the issue at hand happens to be. He draws the other kids into this stuff constantly. God only knows why they continue to give him air time. If he's confronted he goes into a sulk or becomes a blubbering idiot and then there's no getting through to him. If he's ignored he just minces around in his obsequious way and, with me, he keeps asking questions like a five year old looking for Daddy's attention. Whatever I say in response, he turns it back to his mother. If I call him on this, he goes back through the power-sulk cycle again. I finish up feeling physically sick.''

"You really do seem to have a lot of feeling around this one Paul. Have you any idea where it might be coming from?"

Paul gave out an anticipatory sigh. "Can't I just be allowed to dislike this kid and move on. I think he needs to be with a caring and consistent no-nonsense mother figure for a few months . . . preferably one weighing in at three hundred pounds."

Charlotte laughed. "You may have a workable idea there but I still think there's something in all of this for you . . . even if you decide to move away from Keith at this point in time."

"So you're asking me why I don't like wimpy kids who mince around blaming their mothers and looking for sympathy?"

"That might be the question you should be asking but I'm sure there are others that come out of this. Look into your own childhood for a moment and just focus on your relationship with your Mom."

"Oh come on Charlotte, not this again. Can't we talk about a kid just this once? Surely the kids are important in this business of ours even if I'm still stuck with my own experience when the shouting's over." He hoped that she might be diverted.

Charlotte's face was serious and she hesitated before responding. "It's fine to have your expectations and judgements around the kids, Paul. In fact, children need to be very clear about the hopes and opinions of adults. At the same time, how you deal with your issues will reflect the meaning that they have for you, within the context of your own life. Knowing where they come from not only promotes self knowledge, it also discourages you from dumping your own garbage all over the kid. This way you enhance learning both ways. As a supervisor I will constantly urge you to look at yourself in this way. As a person, you can always refuse of course."

"Oh, of course, of course," he said with a smile. "I should

know better than to come in here thinking that we'll be talking about kids or child care, or anything that mundane. I should know that I only come in here to talk about myself."

"All we can ever talk about is ourselves. I'm just trying to be clean and up front about it so that nothing is lost to ambiguity." This time it was Charlotte's turn to smile.

With the preliminaries over, Paul wondered where to start. He saw little to connect him with Keith Potts so he began to think about the differences. The immediate thoughts seemed irrelevant and contrived. He felt awkward. "I have a very loving and caring family . . . ," he began, and stopped.

"What are you thinking about Paul?"

"Just that I really don't think about them very often. It's almost like they're there but not there, if you know what I mean."

"Like you take them for granted but don't really need to have them around."

"Yea, something like that."

"When you think about family, who springs to mind?"

"Oh, my mother, my two younger sisters, Mary and Judy and then there's Ritchie, he's the baby of the family."

"What's the story with Dad?"

"He and Mom separated just before Ritchie was born."

"So you were the man of the house. What was that like?"

"It was good. I had the kind of relationship with my Mom that most of my friends envied. We really were like friends. She let me take on a lot of responsibilities and I felt real good about that."

"So, in a way, you were also taking care of your mother."

"I suppose so but she also cared for me. We were really close and, together, we managed to create a real sense of family. One way or another we kept the other kids on track. We didn't have the material goodies that most of the other kids had and, with Mom out at work, we had to fend for ourselves a lot. We all knew the score and there were few complaints." There was some pride in the remark.

"There was no Keith Potts around to worry about then?"

"No but there were a lot of child care responsibilities for me in those days. Ritchie could be a wimp when he wanted to be but he was only a little kid in those days. I used to take him on one side and encourage him to face up to his issues. This is where I invented my own counselling techniques. I was tough with him sometimes but gradually he learned how to confront life and accept his responsibilities. Jeez, it wasn't easy for any of us in those days but we survived. Any one of us could have ended up feeling sorry for ourselves.''

"You're only twenty seven now Paul. Are you still the surrogate father?"

"Hell no. Mother re-married six years ago; both my sisters are living away from home and Richard is just finishing high school. I'm living on the other side of town but I drop in whenever I have time.''

"Did you ever tell your mother how much it hurt?''

"What?''

"Have you talked to her about what it was like for you to play father all those years and how it was for you when *he* moved in and took over?''

Something happened in his stomach, but he pushed himself back into his words. "Why would I talk to her about that stuff? She's had enough to contend with. It just wasn't that bad. My job was really over when he came along. It was time for me to move on. If she hadn't re-married it might have been more difficult for me to establish my independence.''

"You really do want to be strong, don't you Paul.''

Now he felt that knot tighten and, again, he diverted himself into words. "What are you getting at here? This guy came along at just the right time. Why should I go around complaining about my own freedom? What was there for me to be upset about?''

"The price, maybe?''

"What price? I don't know what you mean by the price.''

"Whatever you lost.''

He lost all that he had struggled so hard to claim and keep—the fidelity of his mother and the respect of the kids. He had none of the authority, none of the rights afforded to other men because they were husbands. He had to fight every inch of the way using his own strength and determination to overcome the odds. The other guy just walked in. He was weak and insubstantial but society granted him the right and the power to take it all away.

He closed his mouth tightly to control the trembling of his chin. He could find no new words to mask the tightness that was tying up his belly. The first contraction of a spasm rose up toward his chest and the thought that he might be coming 'unglued' sent him close to panic. He held onto his breath in an effort to control the turmoil but the pressure caught in his throat. Horrified, he looked across at Charlotte and knew that he was seen. She took a Kleenex box from the table and, taking one for herself, she handed the rest to him. As he took it from her he noticed, through translucent eyes, that his hand was shaking. He was not embarrassed although he was pleased that he had managed to exercise some control.

"Obviously there *are* some feelings here," he acknowledged with a smile. He was able to see Charlotte clearly now and noticed the tear that still ran down the side of her face.

"Do you know what those feelings are all about Paul? Have you really taken the time to examine them closely?"

"Oh I know what they're about. Sure I was hurt when Mom remarried. My role in the family was washed away over night. She tried to reassure me that things would be better with the other guy around but I wasn't going to be anybody's oldest kid. I was angry and sad for the longest time but there was no way to change it all. I just decided to get on with my life.

"Who did you share your real feelings with?"

"Nobody I guess, but that was nothing new."

"Yea, it seems that you had to be the strong one in the family from a very early age. I think I would have felt quite desperate in your shoes."

"How so?"

"I would want to appear strong for the benefit of the others and yet I would have felt very insecure in all of the expectations that I was placing on myself."

"Well there was a time when my Mom caught me crying a couple of times. At one point she thought that it was too much for me to carry and was making plans for us to break up as a family."

"And how was that for you?"

"Oh God, are you kidding? I thought it was all my fault and I hated myself for it. I pleaded with her and set out to prove that I could do whatever it took to keep us all under one roof. It wasn't easy for me. I was never really sure that I could do it.''

"So I suppose the little boy who wanted his Mom ran off and hid somewhere. You rejected him for his weakness and despised him for getting in the way of your show of strength. Even though you knew inside that *you* were that little boy.''

"Yea, something like that.''

"And perhaps you've found him again. He's been around all the time.''

"Oh you mean the blubbering just now. No I don't think that's a sign of weakness. You're always telling me that the sharing of feeling is a sign of strength.'' He flexed his arms to emphasize the point.

"No, I was thinking about Keith Potts. Surely you remember him.''

Within the unwritten child care handbook of behavior classifications, Keith Potts was a 'cling-on.' In Paul's own version of the manual, this category was reserved for about six youngsters who had plagued his professional life.

'Cling-ons' prey upon new workers. They smell the uncertainty and insecurity. They understand the need to be needed and stand ready to make a deal — 'I'll recognize your existence if you become my slave.' Moving in on their target they pull, tug, hug, cry, complain, kiss, vomit, scream and, at times of sheer desperation, will even resort to modes of flattery and compliance in order to maintain their exclusive clutches on the victim. Their precarious objective is to maintain their power over the sagging corpse or hostile companion until a replacement can be found. If they fail to maintain this continuity they become 'floating-cling ons,' secretively lying in wait or bouncing around former slaves in the forlorn hope of reconnecting.

Like all classifications, the 'cling-on' label was designed to disguise the fact that the youngsters so tagged are each different and unique. In Paul's case the cover up meant that he never had to get to know Keith Potts and could avoid having to face the most despicable part of himself. So here was the challenge.

Keith was out in the back yard as Paul watched from the safety of the kitchen. He appeared to be stacking plant pots by the side of the garage but the task and the intentions were not readily apparent. From a distance there was something appealing about him. His tousled mop of red hair, freckles that sprang from the tip of his nose and burst around his cheeks, along with his tombstone teeth and pointed ears, gave an appearance that would have qualified him as a precocious elf in any Disney movie. As he bent down to retrieve scattered plant pots, his shirt and pants separated at the back, revealing an undignified portion of posterior cleavage. Paul smiled. Inevitably, Keith turned and spotted him. Inevitably, Keith began to make his way toward the kitchen. The smile faded.

"Can I make that phone call to my Mom after supper?" He was now in the kitchen, looking up at Paul with contrived intensity. It was a 'cling-on' ploy designed to create the illusion of dependency.

"If you remembered to put it down in the long distance book, you can make your call at the time listed. Meanwhile, we have an hour before supper. How about taking some time to talk — just you and me?"

"Well, can we talk about my home visit?"

"Why don't we just see what comes up for each of us at the time?"

"As long as you don't get on my back about going to cadets. I hate those guys. D'ya know what they said about Charlotte . . . ?"

Sitting in the small session room, Paul decided that he needed to take control of the encounter from the outset. "I was thinking about you and your Mom this morning, Keith, and how much I used to miss my own Mom when I was about your age." At least it was a start.

"I haven't been home for over two months you know."

"Yes, I do know that, Keith. I was never away from my own mother for long periods of time, but she worked six days each week and the only time we had together was on Sundays."

"You're lucky. I wish I got to go home every Sunday."

"I suppose I was kinda scared when she wasn't around for me. I didn't think I could make it on my own. In a way, I'm still not sure I can. Sometimes I look at you and wonder if you're scared."

"Nah! Not me man. My Mom isn't well enough to look after me anyway. The baby has to be taken to the hospital every day, and she can't afford to pay the bills. That's why I stole that bike, you know.

I wanted to sell it and give her the cash. When I first got picked up, it was because she'd locked me out and there was nowhere to go. We didn't have any food in the house, so I just roamed around looking for something to eat."

Paul was not sure what he expected from the exchange. It was the same old Keith Potts giving the same old stories, but somehow it was less offensive than before. He anticipated that the self pity and the excuses would flow for as long as they sat together, but it occurred to him that Keith Potts had actually created a comfortable little niche for himself. He had constructed so many reasons for being the way he was and, through his behavior, he was able to keep people at a distance, particularly those who might pressure him to change.

Keith was still a wimp, but he was a different kind of a wimp from Danny Barnes. More to the point, he was a different kind of wimp from Paul Mattingly. Paul knew that he was about to take more of an interest in his own wimp, even if Keith Potts couldn't care less. Both wimps were afraid but their fears were different. In a shameful moment of recognition, Paul also recognized himself as a different kind of 'cling-on.' All of this he filed away for future consideration.

Now he was free to be curious about the Keith Potts story. What kind of world did this young man relate to? How had he managed to convert the overweight, overpowering, and overindulgent Mrs. Potts into a frail, timid, unintentional child abuser? Was he really keeping people at a distance in order to avoid personal responsibility? What kinds of approaches might encourage him to take another look at his life, examine his options and make some responsible choices.

Later, as they were eating supper, Paul wondered how much more of his own story was reflected in the many questions that he now asked himself about Keith Potts.

As usual Paul arrived early for his evening session with Charlotte. He had spent some of the last two hours with Keith but he was not prepared to report a metamorphis in their relationship. On the other hand, he was certainly viewing it from a different perspective. He was strangely excited and unusually self-contained for a child care worker completing an eight hour shift. He imposed himself upon the supervisor's office without courtesy and was momentarily embarrassed to find Charlotte already in residence.

"Blood and sand!" she gasped, banging her open hands on the desk and sitting bolt upright. "Have you no respect for the dead and dying young man?"

Paul checked to make sure that the comment was made in good humour before moving to the embrace of the old arm chair. Charlotte switched off her brass tiffany desk lamp, stood up and turned to face the night-blackened window behind. Staring out into the darkness she seemed oblivious to his presence and he wondered about her.

In spite of the personal moments they had shared in this strange process of supervision he had come to know a lot *about* her but knew little *of* her. What was she thinking about right now? What did her world look like beyond Willoughby House? Where did she find her joy, her sadness, her despair? He moved from his own centre to consider this woman, allowing his curiosity to mingle with immediate and past experience. He knew that he had objectified her; he still wanted somebody in a position of authority to provide performance criteria and evaluations. He wanted someone to offer reassurance when his self doubts remained unanswered. He wanted someone to chastise him and, in so doing, reaffirm the existence of a world that recognized right from wrong, good and evil, winning and losing, loving and hating. Somehow, despite her resistances and protestations, Paul still managed to sift Charlotte through his own filter of needs.

His curiosity was being constricted by his fear. Fear that she might not be the persona embodied in his image—fear that she might abandon him, snigger and turn in favour of another staff member, plunging him back into a disconnectedness that he knew so well. But how could he entertain such expectations? Why would he want to live with illusions, denying himself the opportunity to know and understand this woman? Was he really curious about her, about himself or even about the world in general? Wouldn't it be better to live with the simplicity of an undiscovered self, the predictability of pragmatic relationships and the safety of the world as known? In all of this he knew that he had choices and wondered when he had come to this realization. Perhaps he had always known but it had never been this clear before. He thought about the kids at Willoughby House. Did they know they had such choices? How could they? Who would tell them or show them?

Charlotte sent a message out into the night and moved quietly to where Paul was sitting. She chose the other large armchair and, with characteristic ease and grace, she tucked her legs beneath her and nestled into the middle of the cushion. She seemed to be in perfect balance and it occurred to him that this woman was as in charge of her body as she was of her mind. He hoped that she would initiate the conversation and she did.

"Well how did things work out with Keith? Did either of you learn anything?"

"Well, my wimp met his wimp and they didn't seem to get along too well either."

"Wimp, take this wimp's hand. How did that go?"

"Well, when wimps get together they soon seem to tire of each other. There's no one to play sympathizer or saviour."

"So what happened?"

"We both sat there trying to figure each other out. When it was clear that we were both in the same boat, I wanted to put another part of me out but Keith seemed stuck. It was like he didn't really have anything else to put out. I tried to let him in on other parts of me, adult and kid, but he didn't seem to hook onto any of them. He just looked disinterested and sank into silence."

"How were you with that?"

"Well the kid in me wanted to go and find someone else to play with but the adult wanted to stick around and find out more. You're probably not going to like this but I *wanted* things to be different for him. I *wanted* him to explore and see other parts of himself. I *wanted* to let him know that there's more to life than wimping out. I *wanted* to tell him that blaming his mother for his unhappiness or whatever would never bring meaning into his life. I *wanted* him to know that he could begin to take responsibility for his own life and that that would be okay. This is awful isn't it?"

"I think it's wonderful. It's fine for us to have expectations of people we care about, particularly kids. It's what we do with these expectations that becomes the issue, particularly when we're in authority-based roles such as parent, counselor, or therapist. I mean, I suppose you could have told Keith all that you just told me but it seems that you don't have too much faith in that approach. So the question is, what do you do? This is where we go back to the matter of intention. The learning starts at that point."

"Well, with Keith it's hard for me to throw off the child care worker role. He's here because of his problems and I'm here to help him to change. He's a kid and my job is to help him to learn how to live in the world and make use of his God-given resources. It's not like he's a voluntary client asking for my help. The decision to do something is in my court. I want to know that I'm competent and if I can get him to stop wimping and encourage him to share other parts of himself then my investment might be more personal . . . if you know what I mean."

"Yes, I think I know what you mean. Since kids rarely ask us for help, it's tempting to objectify ourselves in a role and use the power or insights that such positions prescribe. Father knows *best*, a therapist is an *expert*, counsellors bring about *change*. These are all role-based statements that allow us to use the demonstration of competence in a role as a reason for trying to change a child. They become intentions in themselves. The person objectified in the role then demonstrates particular techniques and success is measured in terms of particular outcomes. This means that the kid should change in certain ways, not because he or she has chosen to do so, but because the adult-in-role is competent, skillful or whatever. Now the kid has become objectified also — an object that should have no say in determining outcomes . . . a 'subject,' 'respondent,' 'patient,' 'inmate' or simply a 'child.' In all of this, we have taken away the kids' autonomy, dispensed with his curiosity and denied our own humanity. In my opinion, this is not a context for growth."

Paul thought about this last statement for a moment. He felt as he had felt during his first supervision session with Charlotte and he was determined not to let his own defensiveness get in the way of his understanding. "Would it make a difference if I really *cared* for Keith Potts?"

"I believe that you do care for Keith Potts. What you don't care for is the part of Keith Potts that puts you in touch with one part of you — a part that you tried to cut off and discard a long time ago.

And if you're not clear about your intention, your work with Keith could well be the surgery that you'd like to perform on yourself.''

"Hell, Charlotte. Do you have to make everything so sinister? But suppose I *am* going to work with Keith on the basis of my own self-rejection, what then? Does it really make a difference?''

"Yes, I think so. By looking at your intentions in the first place, you've maintained focus on the Self . . . upon you. You have learned something, even in this initial examination. Then, if you decide to go ahead and work with Keith, it's possible for you to continue being self-conscious. You will step outside your role and the objectification of the process and take a look at Paul, the person. You'll look at what is going on for you and, as you experience Keith from the perspective of you, the person, you will remain open to *his* experience. If you are open and clear in your intention and experience, you're always in a position to share this with the other person, if you so wish."

"But if I keep it to myself, the kid stays in the dark and I stay in control, right?'' He gave a thumbs-up gesture and grinned.

"From your perspective, yes. But don't forget that the kid also has a hidden agenda. Never underestimate the little devils. At least keep your own agenda known to you. There's always the possibility of sharing it at some point and this is where there's incredible potential for learning . . . for you. If you disguise, discard, or distort your intentions, the opportunities for learning are lost and psychopathy takes over."

"Are you trying to tell me that all motives or intentions are okay.''

"No, but you'll never be able to evaluate them unless you identify them first. Whether or not they turn out to be okay is for you to decide. I always imagine what it would be like to tell the other person. Then, if this seems fine, I make my mind up to do just that. This way I know that I'm going to establish a learning situation for me and, hopefully, for the other person. I know that I'm not going to make myself sick in a world of intrigue and deception. Creating the conditions for learning is like preparing the canvas in the art of child care."

"In my experience, intentions are not always clear. I change my mind as I go along."

"A fascinating process Paul. Particularly where it's shared. This is the process of self discovery. Why not stick with it?" Charlotte smiled and Paul knew that it was time to move on.

"If I continue to pay attention to my motives and I want the kid to learn through working with me, then where do I go from here without getting into the control thing, or simply using the kid for my own ends?"

"If you stay in touch with your intentions and your experiences, I believe that it would be very difficult for you to use or abuse another person, particularly a young person. You will not depersonalize yourself or the youngster. There are people capable of doing this and they are the demons of our profession. I don't believe we have any such people at Willoughby House. If you make your intentions clear to the boy or girl, then you have twice the insurance since there is no basis for deception."

"Oh sure, but with some kids this just increases their desire and ability to throw road blocks in the way." Paul spoke confidently from experience.

"And very interesting road blocks they are. I'd much rather deal with road blocks than cloaks and daggers."

The point was made and understood. Paul nodded his head to acknowledge the insight. "So what then? Now that I've removed the cloak and dagger control and my own needs have been acknowledged, I'm still the adult, still the teacher, still the protector. How do I keep these roles healthy? How do I avoid getting into control stuff and provide the best possible opportunities for the kid to learn?"

"Now we're really into child care work. First, if you stay with my design, you examine yourself carefully in all of the roles you just mentioned. You look at your needs, your intentions and aspirations in exactly the same way. Then you look directly at the issue of control. It may come as a surprise to you but I believe that we all have every right to exercise control over the behaviour of others where such behaviour invades our boundaries. By the term boundary, I mean that physical, psychological and spiritual space that is our own place in the universe."

"Oh right. I remember you talking about these boundaries in our first session. You said that we'd get into this again somewhere along the line.''

"We'll probably keep coming back to it and, at some point, I'd like to demonstrate the idea more fully. Meanwhile, let me make the point that an action by one person that violates the boundary of another is an *intolerable* behaviour. By defining it as intolerable, I now give myself permission to control the actions of the other. As I mentioned to you before, there is no more critical need than establishing personal boundaries. Without them, we can have no clear place in the world. In a sense, we don't exist as identifiable entities, and how can we have health or growth without existence?

"When we identify a child's behavior as intolerable, we give off a very clear message. Not only do we establish ourselves and our place in the world, we begin to teach the child the importance of boundaries. This message will be lost if, at the same time, we invade the child's boundaries with intrusive methods of intervention. As I mentioned before, we need to be clear that boundaries are about freedom and not about control.''

"So we need to be very clear about those behaviors that we will control, try to extinguish, or whatever.''

"Yes. With no doubt left as to which behaviors we're talking about and why we've labelled them as intolerable. Then, in freeing ourselves, we are also being teachers. From a learning perspective, it's important to make sure that these behaviors are not only specifically identified but as small in number as possible. From a self perspective, it's also necessary to make sure that boundaries are set first at a distance. It's always possible to move boundaries aside but very difficult to build them once the territory has been violated.''

"How far can I go in enforcing these boundaries?''

"As far as is necessary, if you're referring to disciplinary measures. You've already made it clear that you won't tolerate violations. If you back off after that, the lessons you teach and learn will be painful. If you're going to get tough, this is the area to get tough in. Just stay clear, consistent and caring. Always be clear that your intention is to establish your boundaries, not to hurt the child.''

"Now, once I've got my boundaries clear and understood, what about all the other expectations I might have for the kid's behaviour? What about counselling, teaching, or even treatment? How far can I push this?''

"I mentioned this briefly during our first session. Just as a reminder, the key difference here is that the youngster has *choices*. Always keep this in mind and, if the rules change, be open about it.

"For me, I begin by making sure that I'm clear with myself on what my expectations are and where they come from. It's back to my own needs and intentions. Then I remind myself that kids will learn what they need to know in their own ways. As a teacher I know that they will learn from me at moments appropriate to them . . . teachable moments. Somewhere along the line psychologists and educators decided that kids had to be dragged down the road of learning, screaming and hollering as we perform our adult duties of pushing their noses against the windows of knowledge, thrusting them against the mirror of self evaluation and barraging them with the judgemental expectations of their superiors.''

Paul tried to place these comments into the context of his own experience. He thought about the years spent in classrooms and immediately recognized the fundamental 'truth' that all of his own learning had taken place at times when he had taken an active part in dealing with the information offered. These were times when he had been personally involved in the process; creating issues, asking questions, making choices, testing options and possibilities. By comparison, information that was passively received, however convincingly given, was retained only for pragmatic purposes such as impressing others, passing examinations, or moving him through social rituals and over personal obstacles. Without direct self-involvement, the learning was shallow, dull and mostly tedious.

The insight that was beginning to unfold was so simple. The thought that struggled for expression and acceptance was the confusing and complex idea that there was nothing new here. He had always known that learning was an active process of self-involvement and that this held true for knowledge and skills acquired in classrooms, families, relationships . . . even at Willoughby House and right at this very moment in time. There was so much running through his mind that he was almost surprised to hear himself speak.

"People learn when they become personally involved in making choices. That's what participation·is all about. Everything else is just reacting, forming habits, coping, surviving, submitting. . . ." He heard his voice drift away.

"I'm not sure what you mean but I interpret what you say to refer to the type of knowledge and learning that comes from inside. It's almost like a force that drives our curiosity, encourages us to look at ourselves, taunts us to become all that we can be, pushes us toward responsibility and self-discipline and then invites us to understand and connect with other human beings. As we move with this force, we realize that we already know all we need to know. Paul, when we find ways to help our kids get back in touch with this force we discover the real art of child care."

"Dammit, why does it all have to be so hairy fairy? How come psychology hasn't given this type of learning the same consideration as the operant conditioning stuff? Why must we always think of ourselves as rats?"

"Well, it does sound a bit like the human potential stuff of the sixties but, throughout the seventies, there was a lot of research that gives support to a notion of intrinsic motivation and learning. Typically, many psychologists decided to focus upon the characteristics of tasks, situations and syndromes rather than the personal experiences of people but since when has psychology ever concentrated on personal experience?" She rolled her eyes upward to register her disdain.

Paul continued to reflect. "In my experience, it's almost like one type of learning gets in the way of the other. If I decide that something *has* to be learned, I seem to lose my curiosity. Then it becomes drudgery . . . like studying for exams or practicing the piano."

"Those are important experiences to remember, Paul. People seem to remove themselves from learning tasks whenever they see choices being restricted, forced, or removed. They appear to have little interest in the task but continue to go through the motions . . . like studying for exams or practicing the piano. Many research studies have shown that people who enjoy particular learning tasks quickly lose their interest when they're offered external rewards, threatened with sanctions for non-participation, or even *supervised* in task performance. So here's some good solid empirical evidence to support what you already know . . . one form of learning really does seem to get in the way of the other.''

Paul's mind was racing along. It was exciting to discover what he already knew and he was fully present in the learning process. "Now what does all this mean Charlotte? How does it apply to child care . . . and will it help me in my work with Keith Potts?''

"At this point, I think you are more concerned with your own answers to such questions. Why don't you see what you come up with?''

He thought for a moment and plunged in. "I still think learning comes from making choices. For me it's at its peak when I feel free to follow my own curiosity—when the project is *my* project.''

"How do you feel when this is happening to you?''

"I feel alive, really alive. I can be tempted and stimulated by what other people or the world offer, but somewhere I need to take the project as my own. If this doesn't happen, the experience becomes tedious and I try to avoid the whole thing.''

"When you're feeling alive and involved, do you know what to do to pursue your own project?''

"Not always but I ask others and usually I find a way . . . *my* way. It might not turn out to be the best way for me, but I discover that in time . . . as I need to.''

"So, based in your own experience of learning, what message does all of this have for child care?''

"Now that's interesting. Sorry, I mean *I'm* interested," he corrected, proudly taking responsibility for his own experience. "I think all learning, academic, social, spiritual, or whatever has the same essential characteristics. I think kids need encouragement to tap into their own natural learning patterns and processes and that we should try to understand how these work for each kid. It's important for the youngster to continue to see choices and experiences freedom in this, even if we're convinced that we know better. We can be there at teachable moments—more concerned with what he or she wants to know than what we think we have to teach. Given that we have control over our own boundaries, we can allow all kinds of freedom but. . . .'' He stopped and became thoughtful.

"But what Paul?" she inquired.

"Oh, I was just thinking about all the programs and practices in child care that resort to rat learning—where we push children into learning and doing for our own purposes. I feel sad when I realize how often we might push kids into doing something that they would choose to do anyway but, through our pushing, we take away their investment. How, for our own need to control, we take away choice and freedom and call it 'education,' 'discipline,' or 'treatment.' I'm just beginning to understand that all these things, including treatment or change, naturally come from inside. I suppose I've always known this about myself but somehow it seemed fine to use external forces for our kind of kids. I realize how much as a child care worker, I've failed to understand that most of our kids have already lost touch with the internal forces of learning and, by pushing more from the outside, I'm only making matters worse.'' He allowed his sadness to show.

"In my judgement, you're being very hard on yourself, Paul. I agree with most of your observations but I think that you're missing an important element in all of this. As human beings, we never stop making choices. Even when we decide to just go along with the rest of the world pushing us around, and even when we take ourselves away from our curiosity and desire to learn, we continue to make the decisions. Of course, children are more focussed upon whatever information we offer them but, ultimately, they still make the choices for themselves. No matter what you do, you can't take that away. If you do that, you turn them into victims and God only knows where you go from there. On the other hand, you *can* be more helpful by using the insight you just described."

"The irony is that, even a week ago, I would have dismissed much of this as permissive, undisciplined gobbledegook. It now seems to me that this is a much tougher, more disciplined and far more sophisticated approach than the old external learning model. In coming to this conclusion, I needed to understand the principles of personal responsibility and communication first."

"I certainly agree that child and youth care from this perspective is far from easy. In my own experience it means constantly being aware of what's going on for me in each moment and taking the time later to reflect on that learning. It means establishing and communicating my own personal boundaries and setting clear limits for the children I chose to work with. Then I need to examine my own hopes and expectations for each child and communicate these without trying to remove options from the child in the process. To maintain my own integrity, and that of the child, I must resist the temptation to take over his or her experience by becoming a saviour, controller, pacifier, or whatever. I need to let the child have the experience, however painful or however joyous.

"In taking my stand of personal responsibility I must insist that the child does the same thing. In this I can't back off, however tempting it might be, particularly in the face of pain, anger, frustration or aggression. I will not move in to protect the child from her or his own choices unless I judge the danger to be powerful and irreversible. Given that the behaviours are not intolerable in terms of my own needs and boundaries, I will intervene only at the request of the child. There can be no behavioural 'targets' designed to mold the child into some pre-conceived object of competence or responsibility.

"And, in all of this, I expect myself to stay with the child, striving to understand, staying with my own experience and my curiosity and concern, always moving with the process, looking for those 'teachable moments' when my experience might be relevant. In the final analysis, I recognize that all of this is for me. The discipline, the tenacity, the pain, and the pleasure belong only to me. It is *my* learning process that I generate, setting the stage for the child to do the same. Here we are both learning together, we are partners sharing a context. None of this is easy Paul. By comparison, behavior modification is a piece of cake."

Paul listened intently. He was no longer concerned with the logic or sophistication of what Charlotte had to say. His own experience seemed to be coming increasingly available to him and his pictures of himself and his work as a child care worker were unmistakably changing. At the same time, there was nothing new in any of this — it all seemed quite familiar. He began to review his beliefs and practices, examining the changing pictures.

"Where are you Paul?" Charlotte's voice found its way into his deliberations.

"Actually I was just thinking about positive reinforcement. I'm trying to figure out where that fits in, along with increasing behaviours, enhancing self esteem and all that stuff.'' He hoped that she would take the statement as a question and she did.

"Positive reinforcement is first an intention. It is an act on the part of one person intended to bring about some behavioural change in another. Secondly, it's an experience of the world speaking back. Thirdly, it's an abstraction, a categorical event identified by psychologists as something that tends to increase a particular behaviour. My only interest is in the second since it reflects a person's evaluation of choices made.''

"But in social reinforcement, our approval of what kids actually do, does seem to work . . . I mean they tend to keep on doing it and feel better about themselves as we go on with our approval.'' He was already responding to his own statement before Charlotte had any time to speak. "But the only relevant issue is their own experience, regardless of *our* intentions. Once we focus on the external stuff, we go back to the rat learning model. Now I'm free to share my feelings knowing that if I communicate clearly, the kid is free to take this into his own experience and make his own choices. There's no such thing as positive reinforcement . . . we're all free . . . free to learn. I think I'm going nuts.''

"It wouldn't surprise me in the least Paul. Three days at Willoughby House is enough to send anybody round the twist. Before we finish for the evening, though, what about your last question? What does all of this mean for you and Keith Potts?''

"I think I need to be clear in my boundaries with Keith and continue to be more tuned in to my own experience. I think I could probably share more of my interpretations, judgements, and feelings with him and learn something in the process. Most of all, Keith needs to know that he made his own choices and begin to accept some responsibility for the way things are for him. Encouraging him to examine himself from this perspective isn't going to be easy but as I become more aware of where Keith finishes and I begin, the process becomes more acceptable for me . . . even challenging.''

"So, do you want to stay with Keith Potts? Do you even want to stay with us?''

"Until further notice.''

Meaning What You Hear

Anna Marie Collinson was a chronically depressed and dejected fifteen year old. She was referred to Willoughby House as a final and desperate move to ward off the spectre of long term hospitalization. The ever expanding case file that travelled with her through the mental health system contained graphic accounts of family break down, physical and sexual abuse, school failure, peer rejection and parental abandonment. Various mental health professionals had described episodes of withdrawal, promiscuity, drug abuse, physical self-violation, and running away. The psychiatric diagnostic profile pronounced her to be "an emotionally constricted girl displaying evidence of Dysthymic Disorder with specific psychotic features."

Paul had read the file carefully. Now she stood before him in the small reception office. She was a stereotypical street kid — crumpled waterproof jacket, faded and torn blue jeans, worn out runners. Her hair, cohered in greasy strands and fell long down one side of her face. With her head bowed and angled to the side, he could see the sadness that all the professional words had failed to convey.

He took the suitcase from her hand. As he moved toward the door he thanked God, and Charlotte, that there were no immediate admission formalities at Willoughby House. The government social worker had left with a perfunctory pat on the girl's shoulder and a brief reassurance that he would return the next day to complete the "necessary documentation." Anna Marie had remained totally unresponsive in his presence and made no acknowledgement of his departure. She treated Paul with the same indifference, but she followed her suitcase out of the office and down the hallway. He sensed that he was being scrutinized from behind but resisted the temptation to turn around.

"We have you sharing a room with Sharon. She's been around here for over a year. I think you'll get along well." There was no response. He lifted the case onto the bed and waited for her to make the next move but she stood motionless just inside the door, hands clasped and head down. "Would you like a few minutes on your own to settle in?" She shrugged her shoulders. "Do you want to talk for a while?" She shook her head. "I'll be back in ten minutes," he said, offering her some private space while creating some predictability in a strange environment.

During his three months at Willoughby House, many new considerations had become integrated into the way Paul went about his work. At one time, he would have regarded them as 'techniques,' drawn from 'theory,' but he now knew that they represented a sensitivity to others made possible through his own state of 'presence.' Through experience, he had come to know that his own ability to receive and communicate information depended upon his ability to bring his own self forward. He was just beginning to understand what Charlotte called the "self-generating principle of learning."

As he worked on becoming increasingly aware in the moment, he experienced a flow of energy that carried knowledge and confidence about the world inside to be transformed into curiosity about the world outside. In this state he could stay in contact with himself, other people and the ever-evolving process of interaction and events. At such times, he felt somehow 'open,' 'healthy,' and 'confident.' On occasion he felt light and 'bubbly' but he found that he could use the same self-energy and openness to express and receive feelings of sadness, fear, and despair. There had been moments when he sensed that his own experience was so in tune with the experience of another person that they actually shared the same moment in time.

Through all of this he was learning. He was learning about the world of people, the world of child care and the world of children as they all came together in the world of Paul Mattingly. He practiced becoming 'present' and now considered this to be his greatest personal and professional training investment. He had formulated the view that all methods of practice could be used as vehicles for the self in action. He was noticeably more energized in his work, less stressed by the ghosts of the past and the fears of the future and, above all, he experienced a new quality in his relationships with the kids and the staff at Willoughby House.

In exactly ten minutes he returned to the bedroom to find that little had changed. Anna Marie was sitting on the edge of the bed with the unopened suitcase at her side. He found himself still looking at the top of her head and, with her hands now clasped tightly on her lap, she was a classical picture of dejection. She continued to wear her faded blue ski jacket and it was clear that she had made no accommodations to her new environment.

Paul paused at the door hoping for some sign of contact, or even curiosity, but there was none. 'Is this real or just for effect?' — the old standard child care question sprang into his mind. He knew that the psychiatric reports contained descriptions of chronic depression, but he also knew that kids were quite capable of using their moods, however authentic, to string adults along. Like most child care workers, however, he was intimidated by psychiatric terminology, diagnoses and classifications. Despite his own experiences and Charlotte's assurances, he continued to harbor a secret suspicion that there just might be certain people and certain 'states' that only psychiatrists could understand and deal with. Anybody, other than a psychiatrist, could unwittingly create personal and interpersonal chaos by simply saying the wrong thing at the wrong time. He knew that he would abandon this belief some day. Meanwhile, he welcomed the insight that the power of any expert is proportionate to the fear experienced by others.

He walked over to the bed and sat down some two or three feet away from the unhappy youngster. "I'd like to show you around," he said, but she made no response and continued to stare at the floor. "You'll need to know how to find the bathroom, kitchen, and dining room just to survive around here. I have a group session in twenty minutes and then, unless you decide to join us, you'll be on your own for about two hours. At least I'd like to know you can find your way around the house." He turned toward her and, to his surprise, he found himself looking directly into her face. He saw her eyes for the first time, and he was filled with fear.

Over the years, he had looked into the eyes of many children and young people. He had seen pain, fear, anger, and confusion — pictures of the life inside. Now, he was staring at eyes that were no more than lifeless features set within a pallid face of wax. The eyes of this strange girl in the faded ski jacket did not look back. His fear was that of a person who turns in a conversation only to find that no one is there . . . a sense of being alone in the company of an other. He continued to stare at the face and felt a desperate need to make some contact, to encourage some response, to confirm the existence of life — if only his own.

"Come on Anna Marie, I'll show you the kitchen first." He rose from the bed and walked toward the door. He was willing her to follow him with all the strength he could muster. He had the idea that any doubts or hesitation would dissect the life force that he was creating between them. As he walked through the door, he knew that she was moving behind him; he continued with confidence, along the upper corridor and down the back stairs that led to the kitchen and breakfast area. "You can always find things to snack on down here," he proclaimed with a casual wave of the arm. I'll check and see if Margaret left some goodies in the fridge." Anna Marie followed silently and passively behind like a purposeless twig momentarily caught up in the eddy of a stream.

Paul fought to stay present during the group session but found himself drifting into thoughts about Anna Marie. At the staff meeting that followed he described his experiences to his three colleagues and they each expressed concern about the newcomer and the prospect of working with her. Doreen, the most experienced worker on the shift, talked about the "seductiveness" of moving toward the isolated world of a "detached" child. There was a place of safety and security in her own childhood, a mysterious leaf house in the woods by her home, where loneliness was taken as an alternative to the prospect of rejection and abandonment. She still sought the leaf house but knew that she could easily die there.

Geoff confronted his fear of losing contact with the world and "hanging out there in the void." He "grounded" himself in words, activities, and routines. Doreen pointed to some of his "obsessive compulsive" habits as additional examples. He started to rock backwards and forwards, to the amusement of his co-workers. Marlene's amusement was brief and superficial. The prospect of working with Anna Marie brought up a number of issues around her own sense of competence. As a child care worker, she continued to attribute a youngster's lack of response to her own lack of skills. She explained her sense of confusion whenever some "unknown" factor interrupts the flow of routine communication and behaviour. Beneath it all was the possibility of "being discovered."

By now, Paul fully expected his colleagues to talk about themselves rather than speculate about Anna Marie. He had come to recognize and value this process as critical to personal learning and self-conscious child care practice. He could have predicted that his session with Charlotte, scheduled for later that evening, would follow a similar design.

"Is Anna Marie for real?" he asked as Charlotte moved to join him at the coffee table.

"If you're asking if she is a depressed and desperate kid, I'd say yes but you've spent more time with her than I have. How are you with her right now?" Paul had been around long enough to know that his supervisor was not asking for any fancy assessment or diagnosis of the girl's condition. Her interest was in his immediate and reflected experience since this would provide the background for all future judgements, actions and plans.

He sat forward in his chair, his elbows on his knees and his chin resting in his hands. He wanted Charlotte to know that he was thinking. "I really feel drawn toward her," he began after a moment's hesitation. "On one level I want to know what's going on inside her head and why she's holding back on us. That part is a real challenge."

"And what's in this for you?"

Paul could have predicted the question and he nodded in acknowledgement. "Oh God, there's some ego wrapped up in it. I'd like to be the person who finds the key and helps to unlock the door. Beyond the glory however, there's something even more compelling that I can't put my finger on."

"So there really is another level. So where does it hurt?"

"Does it have to be painful?"

"No, but whenever we have to go digging, it usually means that we've managed to cover up something that we don't particularly want to deal with. What feelings do you have when you're around her?"

"Fear. I'm really afraid."

"What about?"

"I don't know."

"Anything else?"

"How do you mean?"

"I mean is there anything else associated with the fear?"

He was silent for a moment. "This sounds really weird but there's some excitement in there somewhere."

Charlotte's response came as a surprise. "That's wonderful, Paul. Your excitement may well be the energy that can break through the inertia here. Stay healthy, however. It's important for you to know where this energy comes from and what form it's taking."

"What's the difference?"

"Well, any form of excitement around another person signifies a potential. In a general sense, this is a potential for learning, or self-discovery. It's important to know what the learning area might be. Then, there's the issue of the particular channel or vehicle that carries the excitement. Sometimes we limit our awareness to this expression of the excitement and we lose access to the broader arena of learning. Since the energy is stuck in one channel we can't move it around and we become a slave to it. For moral or other reasons, we may come to deny or reject that particular form of expression and, since we can't re-direct it, we become either obsessed or fixated. For example, if you find that your excitement around Anna Marie is expressed through the vehicle of your sexuality, you may well decide to set up some moral or ethical road blocks, thereby forcing the energy into sub-terrainian streams and chasms. If you keep it on the surface of your consciousness, you can knowingly — and peacefully — move and transform the energy into the freedom of learning and discovery. In this way, you can make your intentions clear and be in control of your actions."

"Well, there may be some sexuality steaming in there somewhere. I've always been attracted to females who give off an air of mystery."

"Simply carried on the pheromones," said Charlotte with a characteristic giggle.

"I'm not sure I. . . ."

"Never mind, we'll pursue that at some other time. Meanwhile, do you have any more thoughts about your fear and excitement around Anna Marie?"

"You know, I have this idea that she spends most of her life in a place where all of us fear to go . . . where I fear to go . . . but it's a place of great fascination. It's down inside, deep down inside. . . ."

"What do you find there, Paul?"

"I imagine it to be sort of like a black hole in space. Like being in a void between one reality and another—where everything inverts itself, finally becoming the opposite of what it started out as. There's life on both sides but absolutely nothing in the middle. Pretty weird, eh?"

"No, not really. Everybody has their own view of what the Pit looks like."

"Tell me, do you believe that Anna Marie actually *chose* to go in the pit that deeply and does she continue to make rational decisions for herself once she's in there?"

"Yes on both counts, although I'm not certain what you mean by the word 'rational.' As people decide to go deeper and deeper, their images and their decision making seem to make less and less sense to others."

". . . and we call this insanity?"

"Sometimes."

In that moment when Anna Marie reached out and touched him, Paul understood the essence of Child Care. She had been in the program for almost a full week and had offered little communication other than simple words to express her most immediate needs. For Paul, even these words seemed to originate and remain in her throat, disconnected from the person within. They had been standing on the steps outside the house and he had just turned to leave for a trip to the Social Services office when he felt the hand on his arm. He turned back, quite prepared to attribute the experience to his own imagination, but her eyes told him otherwise—she was actually *there*.

"Bye, Paul," she whispered and immediately disappeared back into the doorway. There was no time for him to respond to her but, on the inside, he was responding without restraint. As he strolled lightly along the sidewalk, he recalled the experience of his first fleeting back-porch kiss and smiled out into the world. He knew that Charlotte would appreciate the imagery and understand the connection.

Throughout supper and during the group study period, Anna Marie did nothing to confirm any new level of contact or willingness to come forward. Paul was disappointed because he had hopes of a new beginning and secretly wanted the others to know that a breakthrough had taken place. She attended the talk session that evening but said nothing and displayed her usual disinterest in the expressions and experiences of other residents and staff. Then, as the others were filing into the living room to watch the 'late show,' Sharon slipped into the reception office and told Paul that her roommate would prefer to talk to him rather than come down for the movie.

He resisted the temptation to terminate his report writing immediately and dash up to the room. Instead, he waited until the others were entangled in the tentacles of the television and then made his way slowly up the stairs and along the hallway. He knocked lightly on the open door although he could see her sitting at the study desk in the corner. But for the goose-necked lamp illuminating the surface of the desk, the room was in darkness and the silhouetted profile of her face revealed nothing of her expression. Whatever she was reading — it looked like a letter — she seemed to be completely engrossed. He picked up one of the bedside chairs, placed it at right angles to the desk and sat down. She continued to stare at the paper in front of her.

"Hi . . . Sharon said you wanted to talk, but if you'd rather read, I'll go and finish my reports."

She pushed the paper away and resumed her posture. Then she spoke. "I'm not crazy. I just want you to know that. I don't get along with people that's all. I'd rather be on my own . . . just like Graff. He used to paint Easter eggs before he went. He gave them all to my little brother and me, then he cried. They all said he was nuts but he understood us man, he really knew the score." Her voice was soft, clear and distinct, but all of her words were projected at the wall.

"Tell me about Graff, Anna Marie."

"I just did."

"I wanna know more."

"They called him a 'dirty old pig' and sent him off to the funny farm. We went to try and see him but the nurse told us he was dead.

He isn't dead though. Jimmy and me saw him outside in this compound. We shouted to him but he never heard us. He's decent Graff is . . . they couldn't stand that.''

"Is that a letter from Graff?" Paul pointed to the paper now pushed up against the wall.

"No it's a poem." She moved it across the desk toward him. He picked it up and angled it toward the light. It was typed and carefully set out:

> Bang bang, you're dead
> It's in my head
> I watched you go
> You didn't know
> I didn't say
> Not yes, not no
> Some other day
> You watched me grow
> Why?
> Why cry?
> Why lie?
> Why die?
> Why be?
> Why see?
> Why me?

"Who wrote this?"

"Me."

"I'm not sure what it means."

"Graff would know. You're not like him are you?"

"I don't know. What do you think?"

"You're much younger than him. Do you drink wine?"

"Not very much. I usually have beer. What would Graff understand about the poem. What would he say about it if he was sitting with us right now?"

She turned away from the wall looking at a point above his head and raised her right hand, palm stretched out toward him. "He'd say, 'I swear to tell the truth, the whole truth and nothing but the truth . . . so help me brother. This is a love poem, Annie. There's nothing dirty about love. If your father had loved your mother, you wouldn't be here with me . . . you'd be out there with them. And your Danny wouldn't have got himself killed like that . . . and the kid wouldn't be hanging after you all the time . . . he'd be going shopping with his mother. We've got love Annie . . . it's all we've got but, for the likes of you and me, it's all we'll ever have. At least we've got more than them, caus' love's not dirty. It's a love poem Annie. Someday I'll write it all out on an egg.''' She stopped abruptly.

Paul was spellbound. The story that was unfolding in his mind had always been there. Annie, Graff, Danny and "the kid" were everywhere, written into all our lives, including his own. There was his abandonment — a father who walked out and a mother who didn't have time. There was his brother Ritchie and little Sarah pulling him apart. Uncle Marty cared. He understood the loneliness, the sadness. But none of this was her life, it was his. How could he understand her story when the images of his own life danced before him? He could welcome them. He could thank her for the permission offered. He could examine his own and reach out to hers openly, without repression, without deceit. Perhaps he could understand her. Maybe someday she could come to understand him.

He wanted her to know this; that her life was somehow known and understood, but she turned back to the wall and he could find no words to say what was in his mind. He felt awkward and inadequate. He wanted to reach out at a level that was unfamiliar but profound. In his struggle to create words, he lost connection and they drifted apart.

In his brief note to Charlotte, he had requested a 'special assignment.' In the world of Willoughby House, this meant that a worker could be relieved of many routine and group related duties in order to focus on the particular issues of one resident. When he saw his appointment listed in the 'communications book,' he guessed that this would be the topic for discussion. Prior to the meeting, he went for a walk along the back streets to prepare his case carefully. He knew that Charlotte would be concerned about the pressures created for the other staff and he wanted to be sure that his request was fully justifiable.

Two days had passed since they had talked about the poem and

Anna Marie had made no further moves to make contact. If anything she appeared to have slipped back further into the chasm. Paul found it difficult to assess his feelings about this strange girl and struggled with this as he began to anticipate some of Charlotte's questions. Whatever these feelings were, he realized that they were both deep and pervasive. He tried to reach down and through, exploring, questioning and looking at his own life from as many perspectives as would come to mind. He wanted to reach out . . . to touch her world with his own . . . to understand. He wanted her to know of his understanding, of his caring . . . of his love. Somewhere, he already felt her desperation and knew that she would understand his. Her sadness penetrated his soul and offered him life. Her mystery was the blackness that he had so fearfully avoided through his years of survival in a world of 'shoulds' and 'should nots.'

He stopped by the park gates and watched kids playing on nearby swings. Something strange was happening in his life. Paul the child care worker was losing his footings in reality. The anchor points that had formed his personal and professional pictures of the world had started to dissolve from the time he started at Willoughby House. They had come under massive and persistent assault through his sessions with Charlotte and now there was Annie. Now he wondered if he had stepped so far away from the world of the kids on the swings and the old man sitting on the bench, that he would never be able to return — never to be understood again by those who had always shared his life.

For him there would be no going back. How could he now close the door on the being that he was discovering within himself? How could he return to a world of pragmatic expediency, shallow achievement and routinized approval? This new world of unbridled exploration filled him with excitement and fear; excitement about the prospect of discovery and fearful of what he might find and how others might respond.

By the time he met Charlotte in her office, Paul was completely committed to the idea of a special assignment. He realized that this would require intensive one-to-one work and that the process would be personally stressful for both himself and Anna Marie. He also knew that he would need Charlotte as a guide and support throughout the journey.

Her refusal to provide approval and collaboration came as an unexpected blow to these aspirations. Considering the needs of the staff, the residents, Paul, Anna Marie and herself, she concluded that a special assignment would not be the "best move."

Paul was angry, although he could understand the rationale of her position. He had been careful to put his case forward as a 'potential learning opportunity' for Anna Marie and himself and was quick to judge the refusal as a denial of Charlotte's own principles. He talked about his fears around the girl's alienation and the necessity for personal contact to be established.

Charlotte understood and agreed but held on to her view that the people and program at Willoughby House could respond to the challenge without special arrangements. She suggested that Paul could negotiate with his colleagues to spend more individual time outside the process of the group. She also offered increased supervision time. "I think it's time for us to talk about some techniques," she told him.

When he left the staff office, Paul was incensed. He felt controlled, unheard, untrusted and unappreciated. He had made some effort to clear these feelings with Charlotte but they surfaced again in the final staff meeting of the day. At that time, he was not ready to hear that the others actually agreed with their supervisor. He was particularly resistant to Doreen's judgement that he was becoming so obsessed with the issues of Anna Marie that he was alienating himself from the group, and from some of his responsibilities.

Walking home that night, his anger began to dissipate. By the time he reached the door of his apartment, he felt sad and alone. Only after he had crawled into bed and switched off the reading lamp did Charlotte's remark about "techniques" stand out against the experiences of the day.

The following morning he visited Glenrose Junction, a Receiving Home where Anna Marie had spent three short periods of time for 'stabilization, assessment and referral.' It was his day off work so he gave himself permission to conduct his enquiries at a leisurely pace. Mrs. Madeline Partridge, an inscrutable housemother known affectionately as "Polly" to many hundreds of youngsters caught up in the system, remembered the times that Anna Marie had spent at Glenrose. As always, she had information and perspectives that could never be found in official documentation.

Polly had known both parents before they were married. She described father as a "loner always on the fringe of trouble" and mother as a "neglected child looking for protection." Their eldest son quit school at fifteen and became involved in "some pornographic stuff with a group from out-of-town." When his body was dragged out of the Blackstone Canal, the court finding of 'misadventure' left the community speculating for months. From that point, father withdrew into his alcoholism and mother into periods of hospitalization. When Anna Marie and her young brother were not in the care of the local social services, they were left to their own devices; a twelve year old waif playing mother to an unkempt seven year old.

James Titmouse Grafton was a local oddity. Judged to be somewhere in his middle forties, he lived in what was once a storage shed behind the old Corn Exchange. Along with Anna Marie's father and mother, he had grown up in the neighbourhood but, somewhere along the way, Graff had moved out into the "twilight zone." He was known to have been in a number of mental institutions but the local police had always assured concerned taxpayers that he posed no threat to the community. Many of the locals believed that, from his schooldays, he had been in love with Anna Marie's mother and that he tortured his mind as he watched her being brutally abused by her husband. There was even a rumor that he was the father of at least one of the children, but this was never substantiated. It was known and documented, however, that one of his visits to a mental hospital was precipitated by an apparently motiveless assault on the husband after the latter had beaten up his wife and drunk himself into a stupor. The authorities were always lenient on Graff and it seemed to most observers and commentators that "somebody knew something that was not going to be public knowledge."

When Anna Marie and her brother started calling on Graff, nobody seemed particularly alarmed. He used to buy them treats and make them toys; cars and trucks for the young boy and jewelry for the older girl. He painted Easter Eggs with designs and stories for them to take to school. As time went on, his behavior around the kids became increasingly predictable and ritualized. He bought himself a suit from the Goodwill Store and wore it every afternoon to meet the kids from school. He would stand a short distance from the school gates where many parents waited to escort their children home. First he would pick up the boy from the elementary section and together they would wander over in time to meet with Anna Marie as she left the High School. According to those who watched, she would usually be the first out of the doors. She would go straight to where Graff was waiting and then, with a brief pat for her brother, she would link her arm with Graff's and the three of them would make their way down Richmond Road, across the bridge, past the Corn Exchange and into the old storage shed. This routine was repeated on almost every school day and, while people continued to comment, the scene imprinted itself into the composite picture of the community. Speculation about what was really going on was replaced by established opinions that simply became fixated and un-newsworthy.

After a full school year, during which time the school staff reported that both youngsters had made substantial academic and social gains, this unusual episode began to lose its stability. It started with a series of nightly 'raids' on Graff's shed during which, obscenities and threats were painted across the walls and windows. Later, windows were smashed and, during one attack, a crude incendiary device was thrown through the door and onto the bed where James Grafton slept. He was taken to the hospital and discharged some six days later having received treatment for severe burns and having lost four toes from his right foot. During his absence, his 'home' had been persistently vandalized.

Anna Marie refused to go to school and went each day to clean up the mess from the night before. New rumors began to circulate the neighbourhood and it was a popular belief that her father was paying local youths to make the nightly raids. The relationship between Anna Marie and James Grafton generated renewed rancor as public attention was drawn to the scene. Father mounted his own campaign to pressure the police, the school and the social services to take action, and eventually they did.

Less than forty-eight hours after his discharge from the hospital,

Graff was arrested and formally charged with 'contributing.' He was taken to an adult treatment facility in Newberry, some sixty miles away. Anna Marie and her brother were placed under the supervision of a Social Services social worker and a school attendance officer was also assigned to the family. Four weeks later Anna Marie attempted to take her own life. In the early hours of the morning, she slipped quietly into the stagnant waters of the Blackstone canal and, but for one gasp overheard by a diligent security guard, she would have replicated the fate of her brother.

According to Mrs. Partridge, Anna Marie withdrew into silence following the arrest of James Grafton. In his drunken stupors father began to physically abuse her, referring to her as a "whore" and a "slut" who needed to be "taught a lesson for life." As she passively submitted to such onslaughts, he would become remorseful, and his holding and caressing frequently turned into fondling and sexual intercourse. Anna Marie made no serious attempt to ward off such advances. She told Mrs. Partridge that "nothing mattered anymore" and that being father's slave allowed her to go on looking after her brother.

Mother knew what was going on but she turned away, leaving her husband and her daughter to the issues that lay between them. For a few weeks Anna Marie literally took on the role of wife and mother. She said nothing to the social worker or the attendance officer, since she knew that she and her brother would be removed and separated. It took the suicide attempt to bring this about. Even after this, the 'authorities' gave no indication that they knew about her father's behavior, and she made no attempt to enlighten them.

At Glenrose, Anna Marie tried to take her life again; this time with a pen knife across the wrists. In what was later referred to as a "psychotic episode," she walked naked from the facility to a local grocery store and asked the wide-eyed manager if she could open up a credit account for her husband and four children. For the most part, however, she remained silent and constricted, avoiding any dealings with the other kids. During her initial stay she wept openly in the arms of Mrs. Partridge but, after her first period in the hospital for assessment, such expressions of emotion seemed to disappear. Then, following two months in a treatment centre, she closed down completely. "As close to catatonic as anything we've seen here," said Mrs. Partridge.

Driving back from Glenrose it occurred to Paul that his unofficial enquiries about Anna Marie were a considerable departure from standard child care practice. For some reason, he felt the need to justify them to himself. Charlotte had always maintained that "role taking"—that ability to look at the world through the eyes of the youngster—was fundamental to all professional practice. Normally, this perspective would be developed through direct interaction, the personal sharing of experience—but this was not about to occur in the case of Anna Marie. Additionally, he was particularly anxious to obtain some understanding of the world of Anna Marie Collinson before it became completely removed from the worlds of others. Now, at least, he had another approximation; this one drawn from the world of Mrs. Madeline Partridge. With this thought in mind, he turned off the freeway and drove down the side of the Blackstone canal and toward the old Corn Exchange.

The following day, he walked into the staff room with feelings of excitement and apprehension. The day-shift team was still engaged in routines and the room was deserted. He opened the General Log Book and scanned the last four shift reports. At first glance, he saw no mention of Anna Marie, but his eye was then drawn to a brief addendum attached to two reports; "Anna Marie not in group. In individual work with Tony—full reports to follow." He reached over and took the Individual Report Book and noted that there were no entries since his own of two days ago. Instead of screaming, he went off in search of Charlotte.

"Surely, for God's sake, you don't expect everything to go into suspended animation when you're not around. We have no ownership of kids here. Anyway, Tony has experience and skills that are very important in this case." Charlotte was not about to apologize for anything that had happened. Paul, on the other hand, was inclined to maintain the attack.

"Hah! . . . so now you want to talk about 'cases' and 'techniques,' eh? Whatever happened to 'involvement,' 'shared experience,' 'openness,' and all the other stuff that you pump out about child care? How come when the chips are down, we're back to cases and techniques? I suppose you'll be talking about behavior management and cognitive re-structuring before we finish. How about a dash of good old rational emotive therapy?''

Charlotte put the egg whisk down on the kitchen table and wiped her hands on her apron. *"Involvement* usually requires two people to be present. *Shared experience* is both personal and professional, if you chose to make a distinction. *Openness* is a characteristic of all who work here—Tony being no exception. I used the word 'skills' and *not* 'techniques,' but that's okay. When people choose to close the world out, as this young woman has, there are particular forms of presentation, particular pathways to explore and particular competencies that create safety for the journey. Tony is a very knowledgeable, skillful and experienced practitioner. I have great confidence in him.''

"And I don't have these things, or your confidence. Is that the way it is?''

"I didn't say that, Paul, and I don't understand what's going on for you right now. If you're interested in letting me in on the deal, I'd be happy to meet with you in my office . . . in about twenty minutes when these muffins are ready.'' She looked directly into his eyes and waited for his response.

"I'll be there in twenty minutes.'' He left the kitchen and, avoiding any contact with any of the residents or staff, he made his way out into the back yard.

Settled in the now familiar chair in Charlotte's office, Paul began to express his anger, frustration, and resentment. He spoke of his commitment to Anna Marie and about the importance of the issues that were coming up for him. He told Charlotte about his visit to Glenrose and about the trip to the old Corn Exchange, his conversations with some of the locals, and his meeting with Anna Marie's father. He shared his perception that Charlotte had specifically assigned Tony and offered his interpretation that this assignment was based upon her opinion that he, Paul, was out of his depth. He offered his judgement that she had not been completely honest with him when he had first requested a 'special assignment' and let her know that he was angry about the entire process and outcome. He chose not to reveal his fear.

She listened attentively, allowing an extended period of silence before responding. "What I want to say will take a little while,

Paul, probably about half an hour or so. If you want to take that time now, you may wish to take care of immediate commitments. If you prefer, we could meet after the evening shift." She chose not to ask about his fear.

"I'd prefer to deal with it now and I have no immediate commitments other than to let the others know that I'll be a little late for the shift changeover." He walked over to the desk and picked up the phone. Following a terse message, he returned to his chair and waited for her to begin.

"First I want you to know that there has been no special assignment to Anna Marie. I did ask Tony to be available for her and to try some particular approaches that we'll talk about in a moment. I hope it wasn't your expectation that the girl would be left to sit around awaiting your return. You are correct in your assumption that I have some concerns about your involvement, but these were only vague discomforts when we spoke last; they became clear later that night and I had every intention of talking to you about them when you returned to work. In a way I suppose that, in my judgement, you may be out of your depth and, yes, I do believe that Tony's skills and experience are important factors. Now, unless you'd like to react immediately, I'll continue to elaborate on my position."

"Sure, the floor's all yours." His bitterness hung on the words.

"When you first came to Willoughby House, you came as a child care worker full of new training in concepts and methods. Your experience had been one of attempting to apply these notions. I wanted you to know that, according to our way of working, these are only guides and tools to be used in the process of learning about yourself, about others, and about the world in which you live. They are adjuncts to a process of curiosity. Our concern is not about them as things that change people's lives but as vehicles for pursuing our curiosity about people.

"Since we can only look at others through ourselves, I have invited you to examine all experience from your own personal perspective. I want you to be fully conscious of your own experience and the manner in which that experience is fundamental to your choices and actions.

"For most people, this would be a monumental step toward personal responsibility and health. In our profession, there is a step beyond, a step that cannot be taken until we are fully committed to the process of self-discovery and understand what that really means. When we're comfortable with this, we can then direct our attention and energy toward others, knowing that our issues are manageable and that we have the inherent ability to be all that we can be. Then we know that, in extending outwards, we will enhance our capacity to extend inwards. In short, we are in control of ourselves and we have no desire to control others. Then we can think in terms of creating contexts in which others can identify their issues and, in making their choices, move through the process of growth and development. We can consider concepts and acquire skills that operate in the service of growth and freedom and not in the service of constraint and control, dictated by the ego. Are you with me?''

"It seems to me that you've only been giving me part of the story. I'm pissed-off about that. Giving out little bits of information at a time is a controlling device. I feel as though I'm being led along by having carrots dangled in front of my nose. It's just like behavior modification . . . I'm being 'shaped' . . . or am I being conned?''

"Neither. No learning takes place when people are swamped with new information. The sequencing of information is critical for us to see what sits before us. Placing a helicopter before a desert island native, along with a flight instruction manual, would achieve nothing. First he would have to touch his curiosity about the world beyond. Then he would have to learn the elementary concepts of flight, then he would need to acquire the skills to fly. Then he would need to practice and build up confidence before taking off on the voyage of discovery. Of course, it could all be left to trial and error but most desert island aviators would never get off the ground, or would die in the attempt.

"What I try to do here is teach people to fly without being able to show them a helicopter. My intention is not to control by withholding information; it's just that one stage is necessary to understand the other. In all of this there is no deceit, deception, or intrigue. The ultimate discovery is that you make all the choices and can never be controlled by me or anybody else. The ultimate secret is that you know all of this already. The sequential learning process is merely a short cut to what you already know — that you are in charge of your

life. This doesn't mean that you stop learning at this point, merely
that you take charge of it. When you come to realize what you
already know, you can begin to move toward others who are struggling in their own processes. You can let them know, having full
confidence that they can move on and grow. You can learn ways to
do this effectively through the acquisition of particular skills or
methods.''

"So techniques become acceptable if the practitioner is at this
stage. But what about me? Where am I in your judgement?''

"In your own self-growth and understanding, Paul, you are moving toward this position of confidence in your own learning process.
You have done this by learning to be more present and allowing
yourself to be seen by others in a state of vulnerability. You have
given your natural curiosity the permission it needs for discovery.
In this you have already shared much with the staff and kids at
Willoughby House and I believe that they have learned much for
themselves in the process. For this reason, I also believe that you
are well ahead of ninety-five percent of people in our profession. In
my judgement, however, you are not ready to deal with Anna Marie
and her issues.''

"Will you give me more information about this judgement?''

"Of course I will. Anna Marie has closed down. She is no longer
modifying or elaborating the pictures of herself and her world. We
know that her picture is black and, as it repeats itself over and over
again, the blackness intensifies. It appears to be a picture without
hope, without a future. With increasing resistance to information
from others or the world outside, she creates no opportunities for
change. In this sense, her process is well and truly stuck and her
pattern is 'pathological.' At each glance the picture becomes
bleaker and more unchangeable, until she reaches the point of despair where she begins to consider the one option that she leaves
open—self-destruction. If she is to create and consider other options, this cycle must be interrupted. Given that she seems to be
spiraling in the opposite direction, the interruption will probably
have to come from the outside. For this to have any effect, she must
take that first glimpse outside, even if only for a moment.''

"Precisely . . . and *I* believe that *I* had her attention. I told you
about her first contact on the front steps of the house and about her

self-disclosures around Graff. This was enough for me to invest my day off in preparing for further work." Paul stopped himself from saying aloud what was in his mind; ". . . and now look what you've done. You'll be sorry you did that. You should have trusted me and you didn't."

"It may be that Anna Marie was indicating some special connection with you, Paul, but the evidence is not compelling. I know that she has communicated to this extent with a number of people in recent weeks. I don't believe it was a breakthrough but I could be wrong." He felt diminished.

"How do you know this? It sounds like crystal ball stuff to me."

"To some extent, it *is* intuitive, if that's what you mean by 'crystal ball.' I did make some phone calls after our session last Tuesday and found some support for my assumptions."

"You told me nothing about this. My God, we have intrigue and information control in a program supposedly committed to openness." He sounded indignant. He felt betrayed.

"Oh come off it, Paul. Short of calling you on your day off — and you weren't around anyway — how could I have told you? I judge you to be really hurting at the moment, and a part of me would like to stop right now for you to carefully consider what this hurt is all about. On the other hand, I would like to press on with my perspective on Anna Marie. Are you interested in doing this, or would you like some time out?" She meant business.

"No, I'd like you to continue. This is very important to me."

"In your absence, and given my own impressions, I decided not to leave matters until your return. At that time I had no idea that you were making your own inquiries, but I do applaud your initiative. Rather than stay with your own picture, you looked at pictures drawn by Mrs. Partridge, and you even went to examine the scene where the critical events took place. In other words, you demonstrated your openness to new information, even if the primary source of this information, the girl herself, was not open to you. I suspect that this increased your sense of connection with Anna Marie and her story."

"It certainly did!"

"You see, the challenge is to encourage Anna Marie to take another look at *her* pictures from a slightly different perspective. The perspective presented to her must be close enough to her own experience for her to make a connection. If it stretches her view of the truth too far, it will be discounted, since she has developed a solid investment in her own accounts. It must make some immediate sense to her. Once she is prepared to give this consideration, there is a chance that pictures can be compared and modifications and elaborations will begin to take place. Eventually, she needs to change her own story.''

"Does this mean that I have your permission to continue my work with Anna Marie . . . under your supervision of course?''

"Not exclusively Paul. The work to be done is delicate and critical. Right now I'm concerned that you are struggling with your own issues and any blockages here could shut down the entire process.''

"Is this another turnabout. I thought that moving through personal issues was all part of the process.''

"And so it is, as long as you're actually moving. Sometimes, when two people are moving along with their own ideas, a third perspective is necessary to look at the relationship. In this case, particularly, we need to focus directly on the process of Anna Marie Collinson.''

"You are making assumptions about where I'm at.''

"Yes I am but even if these assumptions are invalid, I would still involve Tony at this point. In order to use your pictures to invite Anna Marie to take a fresh look at her own, a very delicate process of blending her 'reality' with your 'speculation' has to take place. She is highly resistant to this process, and there are particular approaches that may help her to move through some of her initial blocks. Once this process starts, the task becomes one of working with her to build new perspectives from ones that have become fixed. These emerging meanings must make sense to both parties if they are to work together. From this work, she can then become the artist in the creation of the life she wants.

"The process is purposeful but, at the same time, it's critical that the practitioner constantly allow her to be the primary creator, that she be encouraged to explore undetermined pathways along the way. This calls for considerable skill, sensitivity and, yes, even some techniques. I believe that Anna Marie is at a very crucial point in her life. I don't want to take chances here Paul, even though I fully recognize that, ultimately, it is Anna Marie who must make the decision.''

"Then what do you expect me to do while all this is going on?''

"Exactly what you have been doing. You may well be the vehicle that she will look to if she decides to move out of the abyss. There's nothing mystical about Tony's work. Right now we're groping cautiously in the dark, and we need all the senses we can muster to find our way. I'd like to have a meeting with you and Tony as quickly as possible so that we can share our beliefs, intuitions, and experiences. I guess I'm asking you to be part of a team, if you can tolerate that prospect for a while.''

"I want to work with Anna Marie, but I certainly don't want my own issues and needs to stand in the way of progress. I've never worked with Tony, so I don't know anything about the experience and skill that you talk about. I'd be interested in finding out more about how we can work together, but right now I'm stuck with some feelings about the situation generally and you specifically. I'd like to clear these with you before moving on.''

"The time is right now for me, how about you?''

He nodded.

Tony Berube was a therapist in private practice who worked at Willoughby House on an 'as needed' basis. Paul had seen him around on a number of occasions but, apart from one brief introduction, there had been no direct contact between them. Those members of staff who had worked with him were unanimous in their respect for the man and for his work. As they shook hands in the entrance hall, Paul took to him immediately and judged the feeling to be reciprocal. In this brief contact, he felt his tensions dissolve, to be replaced by a new spirit of optimism. His 'clearing' with Charlotte had been worthwhile, but he had continued to feel depreciated and resentful. Now, in the presence of this alert young man in the blue sweater, he sensed that it was time to move on.

Once they were in the office, Charlotte invited Paul and Tony to tell each other a little of their personal "stories." Paul talked briefly about his family and the perspectives that emerged from his experiences of childhood. He identified his ongoing needs for approval and recognition and how these had affected his school experiences and his choice of Child Care as a profession. Then, looking directly at Charlotte, he summarized his learning experiences at Willoughby House. He concluded with the observation that such a "personal" introduction would never have left his lips six months earlier. Charlotte smiled and nodded in agreement.

Tony's story was more descriptive although his style was personal. He had been a child care worker for six years before going to graduate school to study psychology. Charlotte had supervised one of his practicum placements and he became enamored with her particular beliefs and style of working. With her support and encouragement, he began to explore "holistic models and humanistic methods," but that which he sought could not be found within the "sterile structures of the university program." After completing the requirements for registration as a psychologist, he had spent two years in various parts of the United States and Canada working with some of the leading practitioners in the field of humanistic psychology. He had then returned home to establish a private practice with a specialization in child and youth care. Now, at thirty-three years of age, he was almost ready to establish his own small residential program for troubled youngsters. Meanwhile, he was increasing his consultation time at Willoughby House.

Paul was relieved and excited when Tony began to share his thoughts about working with Anna Marie. It was clear from the beginning that there was no intention to take over the primary role and that Paul, as the 'key worker,' would stay at the center of the action. Tony would discuss all approaches ahead of time, leaving Paul with the right of 'veto.' Meanwhile, Charlotte would continue to act as the supervisor of the team. Paul had worked with similar arrangements in the past and had actually published a small article in a child and youth care journal advocating for the role of the child care worker as a professional who stands between individual children and the treatment methods of specialist practitioners. He was delighted to discover that both Charlotte and Tony had read the article.

For almost two hours, the three of them discussed Anna Marie from many different perspectives. Paul was amazed—and secretly impressed—with the fluency of his two colleagues in articulating particular concepts and methodologies. He felt a momentary twinge of embarrassment as he remembered his attempts to explain basic child care methods to Charlotte during his early supervision sessions. He realized that whatever else Charlotte might be, she was not naive about professional practice. He, on the other hand, had much to learn but he knew that, if he remained with Charlotte, this would follow his process of personal learning and discovery.

Despite the sophistication of the discussion, however, Paul never felt left behind, abandoned, or patronized in the debate. He shared his own experiences and thoughts and found that they were considered seriously in the construction of pictures and plans for action. For once — perhaps for the first time — he felt like a professional. He spoke spontaneously, listening to the others without withdrawing to consider or rehearse his own comments. He was confident that what he had to say would be both valid and appropriate and that he would not have to search for the right words in order to impress the others. In short, he was a full contributor, without his usual pre-occupation with 'impression management.' In this, he felt good about himself and about his two colleagues. As the discussion moved along, he also found himself becoming increasingly optimistic about the future of Anna Marie Collinson.

Paul's optimism was short-lived. The following morning, he was sitting in the staff suite pondering the oppressive new reality that had wrapped itself around him without warning. The telephone had rung as he was preparing to leave his apartment, and he had taken the call with some annoyance. When he heard the tone of Charlotte's voice, his irritation turned to apprehension and the nausea followed. "Oh God no! . . . Is she going to make it? Which hospital are you at? . . . Can I come over now?"

The voice at the other end of the line was calm. "There's no point at the moment, Paul. She's still not conscious, and they have her under constant medical surveillance. The Doctor believes that she was clinically dead for some time, but her vital signs are all registering now. They're concerned about possible brain damage, but it's too early to tell. I'm heading back to Willoughby now. Why don't you meet me there?"

As he waited in the staff suite, the hopelessness of his own life began to unfold. Lost in the fascination of this young woman's world and caught up in her desperation and despair, he saw the wretched figure of himself cowered and hiding in a darkened corner. Should she die, he would have to find some other corner in some other life. Terror stricken at the thought of moving out of the shadows, he would continue to let others face the world. Through them, he must find his own meanings, his own being and, ultimately, his own mortality. He was not ready to die with this lonely girl. In his own emptiness, he needed more; he wanted the substance that could only be found in the lives of others. For himself, there was no decision to live, only to avoid death.

He recalled the meeting with Charlotte and Tony and the distorted reality they had conjured up together. It all seemed so true at the time, but the honesty of the moment was no more than a lie about the future. 'Charlotte the charleton and Tony the phony' . . . he could think of nothing for himself. At their bidding, he had exchanged his contact with Anna Marie for the shallowness of their deceit and the momentary satisfaction of his own ego. While this was going on, she was drifting further into the blackness, alone and without hope. His nausea returned.

When Charlotte arrived, Paul was careful to maintain his distance, although he could tell she was hurting. She reached out toward him, but he took her hand in a brief perfunctory gesture and withdrew. She stiffened and stepped back. "I need to talk, Paul. For me this is not a time to stuff feelings. My sadness and guilt are all mixed up with anger, and I want to know what's going on." He noticed that she looked and sounded tired but his concern was elsewhere.

"And I want to know what's going on for that kid lying in hospital," he said. "For me, this is not a time for narcisstic self-indulgence." He turned in his chair and placed his empty coffee mug on the table. When he turned back, she was gone.

The resident psychiatrist was not convinced that Anna Marie should return to Willoughby House. Sitting in the physicians' lounge, Paul was inclined to admit that the hours spent with her in the hospital had not been encouraging. For the most part, she had either slept or stared blankly from her bed. Most of his questions and comments had been left hanging in the air, although the random reinforcement of the occasional word or gesture had been sufficient to keep his hopes alive.

Dr. Ben Lipinski listened intently to Paul's account of his experiences with Anna Marie but offered no immediate response. Nestled in the corner of one of the large sofas and picking away at his finger nails, he appeared to be both thoughtful and attentive. When the story was over, he sank back into the velveteen cushions and looked out at Paul.

"I don't know what's best for this kid. We can control the depression in the short run, but she has so many reasons to avoid reality. Unless she deals with those we could be back here in no time. Our alternatives are limited. We can transfer her to the Woodburn Psychiatric Unit, but their program isn't really set up for juveniles. I know that her government social worker sees this as the safest move for the moment, but I'm not sure that it will serve the purpose in the long run.

"It looks to me as though you folks at Willoughby House have made the most gains — however fragile they appear to be at this point. I know that Tony Berube is doing some work with you, and he has a fine reputation in these parts. Then, of course, in Charlotte you have one of the sharpest practitioners in the child care business. From what she says, Paul, you would be the key player in any program for Anna Marie, so a commitment from you is essential. I told her on the phone this morning that I wanted to meet with you and form my own opinion. Well, here it is. In my opinion, this young lady is on the brink of developing a full-blown psychosis, if she doesn't kill herself first. She needs an anchor point somewhere in the world and you might just be able to provide it. But it won't be easy and there could be lots of pressure and pain in it for you. Charlotte believes that you're capable of handling that and, listening to what you've said, I'm inclined to agree. What do you think?"

Paul felt a sense of relief tinged with excitement. He was also cautious in his response. "I've given many hours of thought to my involvement with Anna Marie and I would have a hard time giving up at this point. On the other hand. . . ."

"I know you have strong feelings for this girl Paul and these could be both a help and a hindrance. You'll need the feedback, supervision and guidance of others, and I'll certainly make myself available for that. When push comes to shove, however, you'll be the one in the trenches. Much will depend upon how you feel about the support that's available to you. I know this is Charlotte's primary concern, and I also think you should consider it very seriously. You can't go it alone. If you decide that it's too risky for you at this stage, we'll all understand.

"Without exception, my colleagues at the hospital think that Anna Marie should be placed in Woodburn under a mental health order. A placement back to your facility will be controversial and may well be a decision that will come back to haunt us all. Charlotte is ready to take the risk, but only if you are fully aware and on board. She wants you to take the rest of the day and consider all of this. She told me to tell you that she will be in her office in the morning with time available. Meanwhile, I'll be writing reports for most of the day, and I'd be delighted to talk with you again if you wish."

Walking out through the Emergency Unit, Paul knew that he agreed to the placement at Willoughby House. Given Ben Lipinski's comments, however, he was not sure about using the support system that was assumed to be so critical. Somewhere along the line, he had cut off his connections with Charlotte and had dismissed Tony Berube as incidental to the future of Anna Marie. The memory of his meeting with them had become so remote from his own world of direct experience that he had come to regard them as imposters. He had created powerful resentments around their ability to drag him off into flights of clinical fantasy at a time when a young woman's life hung in the balance. He was angry at himself for having been dragged along and ashamed of the thoughts of professionalism and the delusions of grandeur that he generated for himself in the process.

Quite deliberately, he detoured through the park and sought out the bench where he had questioned his own contact with everyday reality a few days earlier. He re-connected with this theme as he sat down and looked over to the children's playground. He had been unable to make contact with the world of Anna Marie, and there was little in his own world that might draw her toward him or even spark her curiosity. After all, his world was comparatively empty — made up of a few meaningful moments strung together by the vicarious threads of other people's lives. He had nothing of real substance to offer. The 'support system' that Ben Lipinski talked about could never fill the void — certainly not the world according to Tony and Charlotte that began to take shape at their 'team meeting.' He was not even a trained professional. Compared with the likes of Lipinski and the clinical staff at Woodburn, he knew little about the workings of the human psyche and was essentially incompetent in dealing with the distorted worlds of those who grope in the shadows. Since he was neither a person of substance nor a competent professional, and he could do nothing about either deficit in time to be there for Anna Marie Collinson, he had to let her go.

Sinking into his blackness, he rose from the bench and began to walk aimlessly into the park. He was so far inside himself that his surroundings drifted beyond the periphery of his consciousness. He was overwhelmed with the recognition that, at this critical moment in his life, fate had rendered him empty, impotent, and alone. It had always been this way. It was all so inevitable, so far away from his field of control. He was born alone, lived alone, and would die alone. Sobs began to pump out tears. The frantic search for an identity in child care had been a desperate quest for some disguise — a way through which others might ascribe a meaning to his insignificance. The new meanings that seemed to come from inside during his sessions with Charlotte were no more than senseless and deceptive illusions — attempts to fill the void with cotton candy. It was all a trick. All through his life there had been trickery — trickery and treachery.

He stood by the side of the lake staring into the turbid waters, his own image wavering passively upon the contours of the surface. It was drawing him in. There, in the water, he was moving with the rhythm of the universe, the ebb and flow of life. There, in the water, he was connected with all things. He walked forward and the image before him became clearer. Then, as if possessed by some new intervening force, he picked up a rock in both hands and cast it to the centre of the shimmering reflection. The image exploded and disintegrated before his eyes. For a moment he stared in horror and then, fearing its formation or transformation, he turned and ran. He called Ben Lipinksi from the booth by the children's playground.

"Most of my colleagues would probably agree with your conclusion that you should get your own act together before working with another disintegrated person. I'm not sure what 'act' they would be referring to, since it's my belief that their 'acts' are the seeds of their own self-destruction. That's not to say that being disintegrated is an ideal prerequisite for a psychotherapist. In your particular case, Paul, I think you have opened up a fascinating aspect of yourself that deserves further exploration. The critical matter is what you decide to do with it. You could label the whole affair as evidence of your own psychopathology, you could dismiss it as a passing delusionary episode, or you could re-examine it as a fascinating experience."

"You sound like Charlotte."

"How's that, Paul?"

"She believes that all experiences are actually learning opportunities—they're neither good nor bad."

"Yes, I know about her philosophy. I attended one of her professional seminars some years back. I was very impressed by what she presented and how she presented it. Her ideas and practices are not particularly popular with other psychiatrists, but then I always have been a little twisted. It's no accident that I was the one to see your girl Anna Marie. Charlotte always makes sure I get the Willoughby referrals. You should also be aware that she already knows what was said at our meeting earlier today. Unless you decide to tell her, she will not learn of our meeting right now. I want you to be very sure about that."

Paul shook his head. "My God, that Charlotte seems to have her spheres of influence all over the place. I noticed that when I worked my very first shift at Willoughby House. Then it was Tony Berube, and now I find you're part of the network."

"She's quite the lady, your Charlotte. That kind of wisdom, combined with courage and integrity, is very rare. You are fortunate to be where you are. But let's get back to you, okay?"

"Oh sure. I probably stand a better chance of unscrambling me than trying to get a handle on Charlotte."

Ben laughed and then thought for a moment. "In my opinion, there could be many professional and personal gains for you if you're prepared to really take a look at what's going on."

"Yea. I gathered that a moment ago."

"Have you noticed the similarity between your recent experience in the park and the problems that we all seem to be attributing to the case of Anna Marie Collinson?''

"No . . . I'm not sure that I. . . .''

"I want you to ponder that one, Paul. If I made my associations for you they might well get in the way of your own exploration. Can I just leave the idea with you . . . for your careful consideration?''

"Sure, but I've no idea where to start."

"It will come to you as you put your mind to it. Meanwhile, I'd like to draw your mind to another issue. From the story you told me, I have a hunch you're holding out on yourself. I have just a hint that it could be around your Dad, but I'm on really shaky ground here. Anyway, I'd be willing to explore this further if you're interested. Please feel free to say no. You're not my patient and I'm not about to be paid, so both of us are totally free."

Paul had already placed considerable trust in Ben Lipinski but it had been mostly catharsis up to this point. "What am I letting myself in for?" he asked.

"Nothing that you can't get out of at any moment," was the reply.

Ben walked across to the window that looked out over the hospital courtyard and closed the drapes. "Nothing mystical about this," he explained, "just cutting down on distractions. If you take the comfortable chair over here and I move this one just behind you . . . like this . . . then you should be able to relax and concentrate. With what I have in mind, you'll be doing all the work."

Paul sank into the chair as his newly acquired therapist adjusted a small wooden swivel stool into a position behind but beyond the periphery of his visual field. "There's no hypnosis involved in this exercise but I want you to relax as much as you can. Just close your eyes and feel yourself balanced, feet firmly on the floor, back straight. Imagine a line drawn through the top of your head, centred through your body and into the earth. Sense the energy moving easily through you from the heavens above to the earth below . . . and breathe slowly and deliberately. Try to synchronize the rhythm of your breath with the flow of energy through your body. Now, I want you to travel back in time . . . back through your walk in the park, your experience at Willoughby House, your time in University, in school, and in your family. Just get in touch with your feelings as you imagine yourself back at home with your mother and the younger children. And think about how you all came to be there . . . the circumstances that preceded the way things are for you . . . the background to the feelings that you have now.''

Still resonating from the experiences and feelings of the day, Paul opened himself up to the directions of his guide and the images of his mind. His senses moved along with the journey, from the confusion and despair of the last few days, through the excitement of his early sessions with Charlotte, the security and irresponsibility of his university years, and the self doubts of high school. He marvelled at his own strength and resilience in playing the leading male in the drama of his family. He smiled to himself as he observed the awkward little boy striving to move into a role for which he was totally unprepared. He was embarrassed as he looked at himself through the eyes of others, particularly his mother.

With Ben acting as a skillful but unobtrusive guide, he continued to explore the shifting scenes, freezing images and peering into the nooks and crannies of the family fortress. Occasionally, he stopped to describe a particular experience or respond to a specific question but, for the most part, he allowed the collage to unfold without punctuation.

Caught in the image of himself as a young boy struggling to find the strength and competence to be a man, the flow of scenes and reflections began to grind to a halt. The images and the utterances became repetitive, resisting Ben's gentle urging to move on and beyond. Increasingly, Paul became aware of his own frustration and discontent. At first he attributed this to his inability to respond to Ben's questions. Then he concluded that it was necessary for him to explore this aspect of his life in more detail and began to resist Ben's constant pressure to move on. He caught a momentary glimpse of a man with a striped collarless shirt, wide suspenders, pressed pants, and brown leather slippers. The image was massive, towering over him, heavy, pendulous, and persistent. Wherever he turned his face it closed in on him. Ben's voice was relentless. Finally, he stepped out of his reflections with anger. He turned around to face his adversary.

"For God's sake stop pushing and prodding will you. What the hell do you want. This is MY life, not yours. You think this is some kind of bloody game? Get off my goddammed back man." The words and the anger flowed from him without hesitation or consideration. He stared into the passive face behind him, his eyes penetrating, his breathing heavy and rapid. "You push me into this stuff and then leave me to flounder around . . . you just piss off. Then you come in with your goddammed expectations . . . always your goddammed expectations."

The face moved toward him, still passive but firm and resolved. "Yes, you know my expectations, don't you, my boy? You know what has to be done. Well get on with it and stop your goddammed whining. Do what you have to do. Be a man for God's sake! . . . get off your ass!"

The figure came around to confront him squarely. Paul faced the challenge. "You bastard, you fucking bastard!" he yelled, grabbing the arms of his father and dissolving into sobs. Ben knelt by the chair and, in one spontaneous movement, he took the unhappy little boy into his arms and allowed the tears to dissipate into the sleeve of his shirt. On the inside, Paul sensed his connection with Anna Marie.

Down to Business

Patient Anna Marie Collinson was transferred to the Woodburn Psychiatric Unit after only six days in the local hospital. When three emergency admissions created a shortage, Ben Lipinksi signed a release-transfer to Willoughby House. In reviewing his decision, the Adolescent Medical Team took exactly seven minutes to determine that more observation was required — at Woodburn.

Paul handed his visitor's card to an impassive gate attendant and drove slowly down the concrete driveway toward the old red brick military academy that, with only minor modifications, had become a quintessential psychiatric facility for both acute and chronic care. This was his fourth visit in as many days, and his initial fear had been replaced by a general sense of despondent acceptance. The buildings and the grounds were no longer the pervasive symbols of hopelessness. He had seen enough to know that the spiritual stagnation of the place was locked into the attitudes and structures generated by the institutional guardians. It was *their* experience of hopelessness that set the climate. He felt sorry for them. They were victims of their own regimes, following the prescriptions, mouthing the words, hanging onto the routines. By comparison, the 'inmates' were given some permission to deviate, to develop an underlife of their own. He had read Erving Goffman's book 'Asylums' some years before but, in the last few days, the insights of this work had passed from the intellect to the senses.

Anna Marie had been assigned a 'constant supervision' status. Restricted to a designated area, she spent much of her day shuffling around the ward in her pink housecoat and white slippers. Always avoiding the unrest of the television lounge, she would sometimes join some of the older 'acutes' who sat isolated in metal chairs at the end of the hallway and gaze out of the window with them.

When Paul arrived, she was encouraged to put on her old ski jacket, and a pair of outdoor shoes to walk with him through the slovenly gardens that surrounded the buildings. She gave no indication that she was pleased to see him but, on the third day, she prepared herself without waiting for the patronizing coercions of the nursing staff.

As they walked together, they would encounter other patients, generally 'chronics,' whose lives had become habituated to the pathways, benches, and corridors of this gruesome place. As Paul and Anna Marie approached, they would stare or smile from their place of refuge. Fragile, white-haired ladies in flowered dresses, awkward and aimless men in ill-fitting trousers that, in some other setting, might have offered humour or character. Sometimes they would speak with coherent questions or observations. Then there would be meaningless whispers offered in confidence or shouts and screams of apparent anger and hostility.

Paul wondered if at some level or in some way they were all *choosing* to be the way they were. This was one of Charlotte's most bothersome notions. He was always convinced in her presence but doubtful when left to his own analysis of experience.

During this, his fourth tour of the grounds, encounters with inmates were still a source of discomfort. His companion, on the other hand, seemed oblivious to their presence and their behaviour. At one meeting a wide-eyed woman stood in their path, clapping her hands together in front of her face. As Paul planned to negotiate his way around her, she seemed to predict each move so as to maintain her obstructionist position. As his fear mounted, she stepped aside and gently touched him on the side of the face. Only a powerful need to retain some appearance of dignity and control prevented him from crying out and running.

Anna Marie walked on, unnoticed and unperturbed. It was as if she belonged there and he did not. He was known and seen to be different — not one of *them*. The idea pitted itself against all that he wanted to believe, and he struggled to rid himself of it. He convinced himself that his connection with Anna Marie and the other kids at Willoughby House would someday dismantle such notions beyond any shadow of a doubt.

Meanwhile, she walked beside him in silence. She seemed attentive to his comments but unresponsive to his questions. Satisfied that he was being heard and believing in the possibility that he might be understood, Paul began to move inside himself. At first the thought was bizarre, but he felt safe in the presence of this young woman and, while she was struggling with her own inner turmoil, he sensed that she would walk to her own drum whatever he might have to say. He spoke of his experience in the moment — of being disconnected from her and his surroundings and of his fear for this place of isolation. He told her about his confusion around people making their own choices and about his own habit of closing down on experience to make the world an acceptable place. He talked about his session with Ben Lipinski, stepping around some of the details but highlighting issues embedded in the life of his family.

As his reflections became increasingly spontaneous, he became less concerned with the person at this side. Pre-occupied with the world inside, he was amazed when he looked out to discover that they had completed their circuit of the grounds. Glancing back, he noticed that they had passed many inmates, alone and in groups. He had failed to notice them, and they had made no response to him. In some way, and for some reason, he had become part of Woodburn.

He left Anna Marie sitting in one of the metal chairs at the end of the hallway. He placed his hand on her arm in a gesture of farewell but said nothing. As he walked toward the passage leading to the elevator, he turned around expecting to see the back of a lonely figure gazing out across the field of freedom. Instead, his eyes met hers. He felt the blush in his face, the uncertainty in his legs and a pensive smile brushed his lips. Her face seemed softer then usual but the eyes revealed little to him. "Goodbye, Paul" she said. Freezing the frame of the moment for eternity, he walked toward the elevator and pressed the button.

When it was confirmed that Anna Marie would be returning to Willoughby House there was a spirit of relief and jubilation shared by the residents and staff. The kids decided upon a 'welcome home' party and, with some hesitation, the staff agreed to support it and to participate. When at last she and Paul walked in through the door, they were all peering through the kitchen serving hatch awaiting her response and wondering what they should do next.

She stood in the entrance hall and looked around. The "Welcome Home" sign suspended from the ceiling, spanned the full width of the foyer. Balloons and streamers covered the walls in patterns that only adolescent youngsters could fully appreciate. Elvis, Sharon's abused, maligned and much loved teddy bear, sat placidly in the visitor's chair holding six red helium balloons in one of his tattered paws. From his mouth was a large cardboard 'bubble' containing the words "Be mine tonight" in bright blue poster paint.

Paul was horrified. He had hoped to ease Anna Marie gently back into the reality of Willoughby House and encourage the others to reconnect without focussing upon her absence and return. He knew nothing of these celebrations and his anger began to generate a protective response. He stood behind Anna Marie wondering how it might be for her but, from his position, he could discern little. Her head turned in the direction of the kitchen and toward the group of anxious faces framed by the rectangle of the serving hatch.

In the stillness of the moment one face removed itself from the portrait and reappeared in the doorway. It was that of Sharon Hanen, ex roommate of Anna Marie and owner of the inimitable Elvis. She walked directly toward the girl in the blue ski jacket and held out her hands. Paul looked into her face and his anger evaporated. He had never seen Sharon this way before. Standing within two feet of them, her arms still outstretched, this fragile and moody girl shone in her power and her beauty. Her eyes, fixed upon Anna Marie, were alive and direct. With her head held high and her body upright, her white silk dress became contoured in sculptured lines that folded purposefully toward the floor. She seemed ready to challenge any adversity and demonstrate courage to those caught in the doubts of the moment. As Paul reached for his breath, he saw for himself how vulnerability and strength are inextricably cast in the same mold. He knew from deep inside that this moment was as much for Sharon as it was for Anna Marie, and he watched in wonder.

He heard a whisper pass between them and the separation between their bodies vanished in an instant. As the faded blue ski jacket wrapped itself around the immaculate lines of the white silk dress, he allowed the tears to flow without interruption or embarrassment. All he wanted to believe in was there for him to see and be a part of.

One by one the others abandoned their positions in the serving hatch and made their way out into the entrance hall. In a strange and remarkably silent configuration, they drew together around the blue and white axis of the two girls. Paul felt an arm slip around his waist and he spontaneously reciprocated. He knew that it was Charlotte and he also knew that, in his own strange world, he too had returned home.

Paul approached the team meeting with some trepidation. The last session with Charlotte and Tony lingered in his mind, and he was concerned about the unspoken resentments that he had carried with him for the past few weeks. While these were no longer in the forefront of his mind, he worried about the residual effects and the influences these might have on his relationships with these two colleagues.

Once again, he had underestimated Charlotte, and he smiled to himself in acknowledgement. "Much has happened since we last met, and I want us to have an opportunity to come back together through sharing our experiences as they have unfolded over the past three weeks. I hope you feel okay about this, Paul. I want you to understand that it's a way of focussing upon our work with Anna Marie and not an exercise in self-indulgence." There was no sign of reproachment in her voice, and Paul took the message at face value. "I'd appreciate the opportunity very much." He was sincere.

Charlotte was the first to offer her experience, and Paul was struck by the depth and range of her feelings. She revealed her need to be "in charge" at times of crisis and of the self-doubts that often accompanied her decisions. Through the events that preceded and followed Anna Marie's hospitalization she found herself taking responsibility for the experiences and decisions of both Paul and Tony, and she resented them for appearing to make this necessary. When things seemed to be "falling apart" for everybody, she wanted them to "understand" and to offer some support for her position. As she spoke, she realized that this was all of her own making, but the feelings had been there to remind her of old patterns and illusions. She recalled reaching out to Paul following the visit to the hospital and, through her tears, she let them know that she respected the integrity of his own experience. For herself, she went to a sad and lonely place that had become all too familiar.

She had hoped that Tony would provide some of the answers that appeared to be missing. She described his presence as a "velvet harness" that she hoped would stop the world from slipping away. She was concerned that, caught in the turmoil of his own process, Paul would sink with Anna Marie into the darkness and that, alone, she would be unable to save them. "Oh yes, the old saviour is still there in old Charlotte," she admitted. Beyond this, she struggled with the responsibility that was clearly hers, to make sure that the best possible support is available for kids in crisis. Where a youngster decides to take her or his life, the questions of her decisions and her actions were always haunting.

As Paul listened to his supervisor, her central issue began to crystalize in his mind. Despite her belief that people could become victims only by choice, she was a victim of her own competence and her own wisdom. The staff, the kids, Ben Lipinski, Tony Berube — they all knew Charlotte the supervisor, the sage and the teacher. In their awe, their respect, their admiration, or their dependency, they created a translucent barrier through which Charlotte herself could never be clearly seen. In bestowing these gifts upon her, they committed the cruel and abusive act of turning a human being into an object. Through the continued demonstration of her competence, her intellect and her wisdom, Charlotte only added more layers to her side of the barrier. Certainly these attributes were a part of her, but Paul was also sure that they were delicately interwoven within the fabric of a person, unseen and alone. As she spoke, he allowed his sadness and her aloneness into their relationship. In doing this he felt himself to be in a peculiar, but strangely privileged, position. Here was a new opportunity to learn more about this remarkable woman, and his curiosity surged in anticipation.

Tony Berube had stayed in the wings while the events around Anna Marie's suicide attempt unfolded. He had worked on the assumption that Charlotte was very much in command of the situation and, apart from a couple of telephone calls, he had waited for her directions. Although he was obviously concerned about the well-being of the caregivers, he clearly relied upon Charlotte to determine the nature and extent of his involvement.

Knowing this, Paul was even more convinced of the accuracy of his appraisal of her most critical issue. Between Tony and Charlotte, he saw mutual respect and caring, and they certainly related in a manner that was demonstrably 'personal.' Nevertheless, he judged that the teacher-student equation was at the core of their relationship. He wondered if it would be possible for him, a child care worker under her direct supervision, to move beyond his own needs for a parent to discover the person beyond. He knew that, with her, this would be an act of self-discovery, not another exercise in filling his life vicariously with the experiences of others. Anticipating the prospect touched feelings of awe and excitement. When it was his turn to speak, it was an effort for him to return to the subject of Anna Marie, and he felt guilty. He began with this acknowledgement.

Tony introduced the idea to Anna Marie after breakfast. "We call it a Gathering of the Clans," he explained. "You can invite whichever four people you want to the gathering and we will follow your instructions to be as much like them as we can. Then we talk together and, as a group, we try to make sense out of what we're all doing. It's role play, Anna Marie, and you can make it whatever you want. You'll be in charge and we'll stop or move on depending upon what you want to do. Paul will be there, Charlotte, Sharon, and Michael if we need him. I'll try and be the director on your behalf. Will you give it a try?"

Paul looked anxiously toward Tony as Anne Marie turned to look out of the window. The three sat in silence. Paul was hopeful that she would take the risk. Over the past few days she had opened up considerably to the staff and the residents, and she had showed some willingness to share her pain, particularly with Sharon. Now their attempts to formalize the process appeared to have triggered instant regression. Finally, without turning back from her gaze, she said, "I don't understand what this is all about."

Paul drew in a breath, and Tony nodded for him to speak. "We believe it's time for you to take a close look at what's been going on for you. All of our lives are tied up in our relationships with our families, our friends, and hosts of people who come in an out of our days and experiences. This is where we find out about who we are and what life is all about. When our relationships get tangled up, it's important that we untangle them with the people involved. When those people aren't around, this becomes difficult. What Tony is suggesting might give you a chance to untangle some of these things without all of the problems and risks of bringing the real people here. Instead, you'll be with us, among friends who would like to be around you during the process."

This time she turned from the window and looked at Paul. "It has nothing to do with other people . . . it's me. I'm the one that needs untangling. No game's going to unscramble me."

"Maybe not, but it just might be a start." The statement from Tony was matter of fact, with no hint of appeal or coercion. To Paul's surprise, she shrugged her shoulders and responded to Tony directly.

"Okay, but I still don't understand."

"Fine. Let's meet in Charlotte's room at three o'clock."

They assembled at the appointed hour, each revealing their own patterns in their own ways. Charlotte sat in silence, anchoring the small circle with her presence. Sharon, her arm around the shoulders of Anna Marie, waited for the world to continue its assault. Paul nestled into the familiar juxtapositon of his excitement in anticipating the unknown, and his fear that he might not be up to the challenge. Michael, still working through fifteen years of accumulated anger, showed some signs of the fear concealed behind.

Tony was alert and fully present. As he looked from face to face, the group began to assume a pulsation of life, as if to take on its own distinctive form. Each individual seemed to sense this transformation and, one by one, they directed their energies toward the center. When he smiled, they all acknowledged their presence in their own ways. He turned this into words.

"Being fully here today to support a friend in looking at some personal issues is a rare opportunity and privilege. While Anna Marie might provide us with a focal point, we will each be dealing with our own lives and our own issues today. We are not a group of people helping one person. We are individuals exploring our own worlds through our curiosity and caring about the worlds of others. This begins with respect — respect for your experience and the experiences of those around you. Now, before we begin, are there any issues, comments or questions that anyone would like to get out of the way?" Heads shook and "no's" were uttered. "Anna Marie, I want you to come and sit on this chair in the middle."

Standing behind the chair with his hands resting on her shoulders, Tony invited Anna Marie to let her mind drift lightly over the events of her life and to identify some of the key figures. She began with her mother and, as the broad story line unfolded, Jimmy, father, and Graff were added to the cast. In that sequence, Charlotte, Michael and Paul moved their chairs forward to form the family circle. Tony asked that Graff be omitted for the first round of discussions. Gently, he re-introduced Anne Marie to the members of her family, offering some information about each that might help to connect her with her own experience. Through all this she sat in silence. "Who would you like to speak with first?" he asked.

Anna Marie appeared to withdraw, and Paul could not discern whether it was the subject matter or the context that preoccupied her. Since the day of the 'homecoming,' she had become increasingly more talkative and self disclosing and he had hoped that she would continue to progress through this session. He did notice, however, that her reticence was not a regression to the period preceding the suicide attempt. She seemed strained, and he judged that she was struggling to examine and communicate her experience. On three occasions, Tony invited her to relax and encouraged her to breathe deeply into the thoughts and feelings as they arose. Gradually, the flow of expression began to ease from her, and Paul watched and listened in admiration as Tony took her words back to her, maintaining the continuity and providing support as she created her images and formulated her questions. In this process, his energy seemed to move around her, providing ether in what had been a vacuum for many years.

"I noted that you invited your mother first." Tony's observation drew the attention of the group toward Charlotte but Anna Marie remained passive. "Do you have anything you want to say to her? She's here now to listen." He paused and waited, but there was no outward response. Finally he asked, "What are you thinking about?"

"This is dumb. That's not my mother. That's Charlotte. I haven't seen my mother in months."

"Tell me about the last time. What happened then?"

"She just appeared and took off as always."

"Tell me how it was. Where were you and what happened?"

"It was just after they put me in Woodburn. It was the second day, I think. When the nurse came to tell me I had a visitor, I thought it was Paul, but then I saw her standing outside the door. I saw the shape and knew who it was."

"What went through your mind when you knew that it was your mother?"

"I realized that I was her daughter."

"You felt connected with her in some way."

"Well sure. Here I am at the funny farm and there she is standing at the door. I couldn't escape it."

"What's the 'it' that you had been trying to escape from?"

"Her mess. I never wanted any of her mess. I hated it when she got herself into a mess. I never went to visit her, so why had she come to visit me? I just knew that sometime we'd be there at the funny farm, just her and me."

"So how did you feel when you first saw her at the door?"

"Angry."

"What were you afraid of?"

"What do you mean?"

"I'm guessing that your anger was covering your fear."

"No, I was just-pissed off. I didn't want to see her. I thought of all the times I wanted her to be there and she wasn't."

"Like when?"

"Like the time I was in the school play and all the other parents were there. The times when other kids had friends to the house and I could never ask in case she decided to get into a mess. The times when Dad beat up on my brother and me and she went off into her silence."

"Her silence?"

"I called it her 'silence' but she really became very noisy. Sometimes she'd talk so fast that nothing seemed to make any sense. She'd flit from one thing to another until your head began to spin. But she'd never talk about what was really going on."

"So all of the talk was sort of a cover-up for her silence. She wouldn't say what was really going on inside."

"Yea, she just copped out."

"When did *you* decide to stay silent?"

"Me?"

"Yes."

Anna Marie closed down. She curled over on the chair like a wilting crocus and Paul was convinced that she had returned to the black landscapes of her hidden world. He sensed that Tony was pushing—inviting her to carve out new pathways through the "known" topography of her mind. He knew that the story of Anna Marie Collinson had to be told—not just once but many times over. He understood that, in telling her story, she would need to examine the details of each event through the impositions and filters of her own experience. From such perspectives, she might go on to examine the plots and patterns that she used to weave these events into the fabric of her own life. Based upon the teachings of Tony and Charlotte, he was confident that, in her awareness, Anna Marie would create elaborations around each experience that, in turn, would support new insights and perspectives. He also believed that, through this process, she would push out the walls of her prison and discover some space in which to change and grow.

During the exchange between Tony and Anna Marie, there were moments when Paul had the sensation that he was actually blending his own experience with theirs in the emergence of some new and unique reality. It was as if he knew exactly what Tony had in mind and could feel the tension between his insights and the responses in the delicate balance of contact and communication. There were times when he moved as if he were Tony, listening, reflecting, and challenging with perspectives that seemed to spring up without warning. He had no doubt that they were both equally involved. In the same moment, he would live in the world of Anna Marie, not as a response to Tony but as an independent, yet converging reality. Again, this information seemed to present itself without conscious effort. He had constructed many pictures and images but, taken together or in isolation, they could not account for the richness of these momentary glimpses. He was aware that he had closed down with her, and he knew why.

At yet another level, Paul was always conscious of the integrity of his own thoughts and feelings as they saturated and embraced each moment in time. He knew the wisdom of Charlotte's cliche that we are all "the stars in our own show." He also knew that skilled interpersonal work could be a highly creative process, capable of transforming the beliefs and experiences of those involved.

Somewhere along the line, however, he was losing touch with many of the core issues and practices of child care, and he made a mental note to attend to these at some future time.

"So you felt a lot of resentment when you saw your mother standing at the door. What did you do with that feeling?"

Anna Marie maintained her wilting posture but honoured the relative safety of the question with a response. "I didn't do anything. I just turned away."

"So you stuffed the feeling and said, 'I refuse to speak with you, mother, but I won't tell you why.'"

"Yea, I guess so."

"Will you tell *me* why?"

"Why what?"

"Why you refused to tell your mother about your anger and your resentment toward her."

"Because I don't want to get sucked in, that's why."

"You don't want to get sucked into what? What could she draw you into?"

"Her goddammed mess . . . her goddamned mess." She sat upright in her chair and looked directly at Tony.

"You're scared of her mess aren't you Anna Marie? You're scared of what it means for you . . . aren't you?"

She leaned forward with a sense of urgency that Paul had never seen before. "You're goddammed right I'm scared. I don't want to get into that stuff," she replied with startling ferocity.

"Why not. What are you scared about?"

"I'm not like her. God, I did all the things she couldn't do. Everybody knows I'm not like her. I've got nothing left to say to her. We're miles apart . . . completely different."

"And she thinks that you and she are the same?"

"Yes . . . because it gets her off the hook. She makes me out to look like her to get away from her own stuff, from her own goddammed mess."

"And how do you feel about this?"

"Pissed-off." The expression spat from her lips.

"What do you want to say to her about it? She'll listen to what you have to say now." He pointed toward Charlotte.

"I want you to let me be myself." Her voice was quiet and subdued.

"Tell her so she can really hear you. Let her know your feelings about it, Anna Marie."

Paul noticed that she was trembling as she looked in Charlotte's direction. It was Charlotte who spoke. "You really want to be like me, don't you?"

Anna Marie clenched her fists and stopped breathing. Paul also stopped breathing. The pressure mounted in each of them. Paul opened his mouth but it was Anna Marie who screamed, "No! . . . No! . . . No!. . . ."

Drinking tea in the familiar world of Charlotte's office, the three core team members reflected on the afternoon session. Paul was secretly impressed with the progress that had been made but, rather than be seen as a wide eyed neophyte in the arena of psychotherapy, he acknowledged the cautionary comments of his colleagues with appropriate professional cliches and affirmations. Eventually, Tony turned to him directly. "Since you'll be doing much of the work between sessions, Paul, I'd like to share my thoughts and observations for your consideration. It will take a few minutes. Do you have time now?"

"Sure I'd also like to know a little more about the approaches you used today."

Tony placed his cup on the table with careful precision and, as their eyes met, Paul became immediately aware of himself as the focal point of attention. In that moment, he caught a personal glimpse of Tony, the therapist. "Basically, Paul, I'm inviting Anna Marie to look at specific events in her life and re-examine these within the network of threads that she uses to weave them together. For most people, the process of living everyday provides sufficient challenge for them to examine and reflect on experiences as they create their meanings of who they are in the world. Anna Marie is well and truly 'stuck,' and this thing called 'therapy' is to encourage her to take a risk and look again, rather than die in the unchanging dungeon that she's built for herself. Ultimately, we hope that she will re-assess the threads, or meanings, that hold her life together, but our initial approach is through the content of her experience — the details of the day-to-day incidents that provide the grist for the unfolding story. The key to change lies in her recounting of these details, not in the creation of sweeping or dramatic insights that will transform despair into euphoria. In revealing the nuts and bolts of experience she, and we, can begin to look at how she constructs her life, and we can offer encouragement and support in modifying structures and meanings. Additionally, in the sharing of the stories, Anna Marie re-connects her life with others. Our presence is crucial.

"It's a slow and rigorous process, and it may be necessary for each part of the story to be told many times, from many perspectives, in many versions, before she makes any truly significant discovery. Even then, the process of change is still at an embryonic stage. Next she must transpose such insights or discoveries into actions — different ways of thinking or doing that will serve to give her a sense of freedom and well-being in the world. Here she begins to assume authorship for her life. This is the struggle where efforts to change can quickly become disillusions. Here is where the day-to-day support of child care work will be critical. Then, there's the process whereby she will assimilate these new beliefs and actions into her view of who she is in the world — the stage where we will need to offer our feedback and our affirmations. Finally, she will be able to fully integrate these features into her spontaneous perception and presentation of herself.

"So you see how gradual, systematic, and integrated this whole process becomes, how day-to-day child care work blends with the episodal effects of individual therapy sessions. It always amuses me when I hear child care workers derogate themselves for being immersed in the pushes and pulls of everyday life. These are the very things that we're trying to tap into with Anna Marie as we try to create a new foundation for learning. As we move on, I hope that we will be giving her specific homework at all levels . . . affective, cognitive, and behavioral. This is where some of the regular child care practices can be incorporated into a framework that's being constructed by her, as a person in her own right, and not by the expectations of the worker or the demands of the moral majority."

"How do you know where to begin and where to stop?" asked Paul.

"She determines both. As we work more together, you'll notice that I will always begin by asking her to talk about what's important for her. I will always finish by asking her if that's what she wants."

"Yes, but you do have some sense of direction in mind."

"I have some general story lines to work on, but I want her to do most of the work and I'm quite happy to follow behind. I concentrate on my curiosity about her. If I become overly concerned with doing the 'right' thing as a therapist, then I lose my fascination with *her*. If I become too concerned with the themes of her story, then I lose interest in the details of her experience. In this way, I also lose interest in *her* and our contact collapses."

"But if you immerse yourself in the details, surely you become lost in the trivia of it all, like chit-chat in a laundromat," Paul suggested.

"If you stay with the detail, it could certainly end up in a meaningless mass of images and verbiage. On the other hand, if there's no interest in these immediate pictures, there's no foundation from which to construct new ones. Ultimately, our task is to return to the core of self and existence that transcends the experience, and even the interpretation, of events. As a fellow Charlotte student, I'm sure you know what I'm talking about."

They exchanged knowing glances and Paul pushed the dialogue along. "Some parts of the session this afternoon were quite dramatic. Does this tend to move the process along?"

"It can, Paul, but it's just one part of the process. As you know, pain is never dramatic. The drama begins when the story begins to move toward the pain. The climax comes when the pain is expressed and the 'denouement' integrates the experience into a new phase of life. Drama, in itself, has its value in the moment, but it takes its meaning from a much more protracted and complex process, occurring within the context of a total life. For the complete story to unfold, we need the facts *and* the feelings. As you know from your child care experience, the totality is built upon, and discovered within, the bits and pieces of daily life."

"So, do you have any insights or observations in the case of Anna Marie Collison?"

"Well, we've already talked about many things, and I know that you and Charlotte have shared a lot of thoughts and ideas. Let me just throw a few extra notions into the hat. Unlike Charlotte, who is able to carry six stories at once, I tend to stay with one basic story line that I modify as I go along. Please know that this is not a pretense at a diagnosis, just an ever-changing framework to hang my experience on.

"From here, I construct my own impressions and create my own insights to share in the co-creation of the encounter. I never assume that I know more than the other, in this case Anna Marie, and I constantly change the plots and the patterns as the story begins to unfold. In this particular case, there's just a hint of a story in the air and I'm grasping for its most general character and flavor.

"As the main protagonist, I have a young girl who is scared to live a life that seems pre-ordained toward loneliness and despair. Her father, older brother, and mother disconnected themselves through alcohol, suicide, and mental illness, and the family as a whole generated little evidence to suggest that things could be any different. In the session this afternoon, her conviction that she is essentially the same person as her mother was not seriously challenged by her protestations to the contrary. 'I saw the shape and knew who it was' seems to confirm the inevitability of mother and the 'mess' that they must always share.

"A long time ago, Anna Marie chose to accept her fate and closed off, but she found some tenuous sense of purpose in protecting her little brother: *he* might have a chance. Then she met this man Graff. He was contactable because he too was a loner. But old Graff had one very different and distinctive quality. Somewhere along the lonely road, he had discovered some joy in his life. It could also be that he hadn't given up completely on the prospect of connecting with others, and Anna Marie was drawn to the challenge.

"As my very tentative picture begins to take shape, I have an idea that Anna Marie confirms her unhappy present and bleak future through talking with others. As the images of what is, and what is to be, assume their inevitable blackness, she begins to back away from that which she fears the most. First she stops talking, and then she constructs the impermeable barrier between herself and those who might apply the final devastating brush strokes. She sits precariously on the edge, not daring to look. As the ground slips away beneath her feet, she may decide to leap blindly into the abyss rather than look into the blackness.

"I have dreams about that kind of choice," Paul interjected.

"I think that it's universally symbolic of many dilemmas. In Anna Marie's case, it's acted out directly in the drama of her life. It is literally a stance between life and death."

"If your metaphor is valid, there will be no resolution to the dilemma until she opens her eyes and takes a look into the void — until she actually confronts her greatest fears." Paul suggested.

"Yes, she must make a conscious *choice* to live. Remember, however, that we are now approaching the story with very broad perspectives and sweeping speculations. If the details that we flesh out in the sessions, or in your individual work, serve to support such perspectives, the chances are that we will still have a long way to go. The microcosms of the dilemma are contained in the relationships with others and in the internal dialogues that take place within her own world of personal experience. In the course of the sessions, I will be encouraging her to bring these dialogues out into the open, inviting parts of the self to talk to one another. I believe that failure to communicate is as much a matter of internal integration as social integration. As this proceeds, our present story line may change dramatically as the various events, plots, and sub-plots reveal themselves. In the end, there may be no dramatic scene with Anna Marie standing fearfully and then majestically looking out over the abyss. This peering into the unknown may occur incrementally in a hundred episodes as the fear dissipates, almost imperceptibly."

"Now it comes back to me!" Paul explained, slapping his knee in a gesture of sudden understanding. You're talking about Gestalt Therapy. It was big stuff in the '60s and '70s wasn't it?"

"You're right on Paul," Charlotte acknowledged, breaking her prolonged silence. "Some of the contact and communication approaches were devised and developed by Fritz Perls and his colleagues as far back as the fifties. It was an attempt to put therapeutic action into the more passive psychoanalytic arena. In Tony's work, many of these ideas and approaches are incorporated into his own humanistic style, along with many other things, of course." She had their attention.

"Since I've already interrupted, I'd like to carry on to underscore how the team concept works here. In the first place, the orientation draws our curiosity to Anna Marie as a person, and it's her experience that drives the process along. We're not bound by our theories and blindly invested in our techniques or their apparent outcomes. It's this perspective that allows us to stay humanistic and avoid the dangers of becoming mechanistic. Secondly, we are concerned with all aspects of her experience, recognizing that discovery and change can occur in the kitchen as much as in the session room. Thirdly, the story of Anna Marie Collinson that is written at Willoughby House will be re-written many times over in the years to come. As a team, we are not seeking absolute truth, so there's no issue of one person being right and another wrong. Even if a particular insight is validated through Anna Marie herself, it doesn't make it right; we simply register agreement.

"I'm making this little speech because the four of us have never worked together before, and I find it neat to recognize the freedom that we have to collaborate and value our individual contributions. Is it really possible for a child care worker, his supervisor, a consulting psychologist, and a very unhappy fifteen year old girl to work in this way? You're probably tired of hearing the replays, Paul, but I believe that all of the learning is enfolded within our experience and that it will emerge as we unfold our experiences together. So, yes, I think that all this is possible, but only if we are prepared to identify and confront our own issues as we move along. In doing this, I believe that we will be doing no more, and no less, than we hope for our sad little girl out there. In the final analysis, our individual issues are universal and the recognition and resolution can only come through contact and communication with ourselves and with others."

Charlotte rose from her chair and beamed at her two colleagues. "Where would I be without my little speeches?" she asked. Then, with the gentleness of an Oriental rose, she kissed each one on the cheek and disappeared through the door and down the hallway.

Back to Basics

Tomorrow, my meeting with Charlotte will have a very special focus. After six months at Willoughby House, it is time for me to write an evaluation of my work in the program. Taking this responsibility for myself is quite a challenge — a totally different experience from the usual anticipation of being judged, tagged, and patronized by a superior. I was skeptical at first, but I now have some confidence in this idea of self-evaluation, and I know that Charlotte's own comments and observations won't blow me out of the water. Although I still have much to learn, the perceptions and judgements of my colleagues are well known to me, and I feel quite safe in letting them know what's happening from my perspective.

The policy manual describes these formal evaluations as "opportunities to consolidate and integrate learning." While the focus is on the experience of the individual staff member, it is made clear that Charlotte reserves the right to add her own observations before the document becomes part of official agency records. It's important for me to note that no member of staff can recall a time when she chose to exercise this right. It would certainly be difficult for any practitioner to reach a six-month evaluation and be in profound disagreement with Charlotte's judgements and perceptions. Usually, she will defer to a person's own self-perceptions.

As I sit here in anticipation, I'm also aware that I will be invited to share my evaluative deliberations with the staff group and that they will be free to respond. I've already participated in the evaluations of two other staff members and know how lively these sessions can be. This is a particular blend of feelings that has become so much a part of my Willoughby House experience.

Looking around my messy little living room, I see nothing that gives particular significance to the last six months. Obviously, I'm just as messy as ever but, as a child care worker and as a person,

I've made some major shifts in my thinking and my behavior. I want to be clear about these before tomorrow's meetings.

I know that there's no difference between Paul the person and Paul the child care worker but, even now, the implications of this innocent little notion can take me by surprise at any moment, day or night. Whenever, I want to avoid pain, guilt, dissonance, or whatever, I'm still tempted to detach myself from what I'm doing and put up the barriers to prevent the person from communicating with the actor. Sometimes I succumb to the temptation, even though I know that the price is to substitute stagnation for learning. Just like the kids I work with, my growth and development take place as I allow myself to fully participate in the events of my life and to reflect on my own experience in creating purpose and meaning. These words would have sounded strange six months ago, but here I am running them through my mind without hesitation.

I am now firm in my belief that Child Care really is an under-developed and under-valued profession — particularly by those who claim to practice it. For years, I've heard the 'experts' broadcast cliches to this effect but, for some reason, I always detected a hollow and patronizing tone in their words. While advocating on behalf of the Child Care Association, or presenting my perspectives at case conferences, there was always an underlying suspicion that something called 'therapy' conducted by someone called a 'therapist' was the ultimate ritual for growth and change.

During my early 'unlearning' sessions with Charlotte, I took the freedom she offered to debunk the whole idea of psychotherapy outright, in order to promote the process of honesty and open exchange between worker and youngster. Now I believe that it *is* possible for a well-intended and experienced person to develop particular styles and use particular approaches to invite a youngster to examine personal experience, confront blocks or fears, and take the risk to move on. This can be done without sacrificing the self for the role, or integrity for technique.

If this is therapy, then it belongs to the field of Child and Youth Care. It's a process that takes place where the raw experience of the adult merges with the raw experience of the child, and not an arena of lofty concepts and fancy ideas. We build from moments of personal contact and reflection in the ever grinding mill of everyday life. Children, in particular, learn through content before abstractions. Every moment, every detail, every action, thought, and feeling provides the grist for their creations. Among all the helping professionals, only child and youth care workers have the courage and the privilege to immerse themselves in the everyday life world of their 'clients.' If they can take the risk to be themselves and acquire the skills and confidence to speak directly to the youngsters in their care, they can become therapists par excellence. By comparison, those who would question their credibility would become no more than empty voices on the wind.

There was a time when my training established my identity as a child care worker. Realizing that my effectiveness is based upon my openness to learn from personal experience, I suspect that the training I received took me in the opposite direction. Presenting the false confidence of theories and the shallow competence of controlling practices, it was easy for me to hide from myself and from the world. In that place, I deny myself the pleasures and pains of learning and take on the 'anesthesia of the expert.' It seems that the more I advocated for myself and my colleagues as 'experts,' the more I closed off to the vulnerability of personal learning and sought the trimmings and trappings of the role.

And I'm 'just' a child care worker. I can imagine how seductive all this would be for a Ph.D. — to assume the mantle of 'expert on human affairs' at the age of twenty three when his or her own humanity has never been explored. I can see how the disguise might blossom while the neophyte self slowly dies on the inside. Surely, the longer this goes on, the more difficult it becomes for the self to speak back. And here is our 'expert' facilitating the self-actualization of others. Over the years, I've met so many high status professionals who seem unable to reach out beyond their words and to cast aside the repetitious shackles of their roles. Having held such people in awe for so long it's strange for me to view them with compassion. Whatever else occurs, I know that I've abandoned my envy of them forever.

I still want to be a professional and a student of child care. I want to create my own experiences and perspectives, while striving to understand the experiences and perspectives of others. In this, I want to value what Anna Marie has to offer as much as I value the

writing of Jean Piaget, the skills of Tony, or the wisdom of Charlotte. I want to discover ways to help kids explore their resources
and integrate their lives as I experience and explore the child within
me. In child care, I have full permission to learn cognitively
through communication with others, I have constant opportunities
to meet my emotional needs as I offer and receive caring and love
and, at the behavioural level, I'm always challenged to demonstrate
competence, autonomy, and self-worth.

This is a very different project from the one that I started out
with. In preparation for tomorrow, I need to be clear about how
basic child care practices blend with my changing orientation. I still
feel embarrassed when I remember some of my early presentations
to Charlotte, but some things haven't changed. For me, child care is
still a process of teaching, and issues of control, authority, and
responsibility cannot be neatly tucked away behind a floral screen
of humanistic ideology.

I still believe that discipline is the pivotol issue in Child and
Youth Care. Unless a youngster learns to control impulses and de-
lay immediate gratification in the interest of priorities and future
possibilities, there is no real foundation for systematic learning and
responsible action.

In all societies, adults have a fundamental obligation to teach this
ability to children in the context of the unique values and qualities
of their particular culture. In our society, I have every right to encourage certain behaviours and discourage others within the framework of social expectations and the protection of personal boundaries. Hence, I would be violating my own integrity by allowing a
child to steal candy or to invade my personal space. I would never
protect a child from the natural consequences of his or her actions
and, in a child care setting, I might see to it that such consequences
actually occur. Ultimately, it is my hope that each child will find a
safe pathway to personal growth within the context of society, and
it's my job to teach the expectations as well as the skills that make
for responsible action.

I used to believe that discipline was an externally imposed framework, internalized in habit or conscience and expressed through
rituals and guilt. I now believe that discipline is an internally generated need, externalized in choice or responsibility and expressed

through spontaneity and freedom. Hence, I no longer entertain the prospect of 'disciplining' a child. Rather, I might apply particular consequences in order to encourage a youngster to examine, or evoke, his or her own self-disciplinary resources.

On the surface, the practices might appear to be identical, but the intent is quite different. With the self-directed approach, I am not interested in focussing upon the suppresive power of the external world. My intention is to offer information from which the boy or girl knows that there are choices to be made. Since my interest is in the application of internal controls, I will naturally look beyond the behaviour to discover what the youngster sees and whether the discipline is an act of freedom or a response to perceived control. Additionally, I want to know what feeling he or she associates with the act. So my technique and the behavioral outcome might appear as external control but, in my concern with the cognitive and the affective, and in my ongoing contact with the youngster, the quest is to explore freedom rather than create an experience of control.

Whenever I establish a rule, a personal boundary or an expectation, and associate these with consequences to the youngster, I realize that I'm still doing 'behavioral intervention.' The difference is that my real concern is not with the behavioral outcome but with the reasons that the youngster gives to himself or herself for deciding to behave in that particular way.

By sitting down to talk about this I achieve a number of objectives. In the first place, my curiosity lets the youngsters know that my interest is in them and their experience. Secondly, I invite them to bring their decision making to a conscious level, which promotes personal autonomy and responsibility. Thirdly, I begin to get a sense of whether they believe that they are actually making choices, or merely see themselves as victims of an oppressive world. Where they assume the latter perspective — and this is common in my experience — I then know that I have more work to do in teaching them the skills and introducing the beliefs that offer freedom from this self-imposed prison.

I like to think of this as discipline 'from the inside out.' At the broadest level, discipline becomes a pathway to personal freedom and responsibility. I never thought of it this way when I did my early training in behavior management and control. Then again, I never really thought about it.

I still believe that 'caring' is the essential quality of child care, but I'm less inclined to allow my caring to become transformed into an overwhelming sense of responsibility. I'm still struggling to find my place in this one, however.

Accepting personal responsibility for my own actions, and knowing that I can never be responsible for the actions or decisions of a child, is a useful working principle but, for me, it still translates into day-to-day dilemmas. When Anna Marie was seriously considering taking her life, I would have done anything to prevent her from doing so. Had she succeeded, there is no doubt that I would have found some way to hold myself responsible. Now that she is gradually re-examining her experience and accepting life more and more as a personal challenge, the issue isn't as pressing, but it is still there. Now it appears more through my need for her to move along with her life. Whenever I see her making changes that we have anticipated in our sessions together, I want to take some of the credit, and this implies taking some of the responsibility. Reminding myself that she takes responsibility for her actions and I take responsibility for mine doesn't really make it clean. Meanwhile, I'll live with Charlotte's suggestion that I use the reminder as a point of reference — a sort of personal check on my own needs to care and control.

In my experience, open expressions of caring are often discouraged among practitioners. I worked in one residential program where an admission of caring was considered to be a sign of weakness. More frequently, however, the suppression of caring behavior seems to relate to some archetypal concept of the seasoned child care worker as a tough-minded, in-charge individual, always ready to pounce on the first sign of manipulation and to courageously confront the inappropriate. From this perspective, even listening to a child's story may be viewed as 'feeding into' the problem. For similar reasons, doing something *for* the child — making the bed, phoning a friend, making a small gift — is frowned upon as an act that buys 'favors' for the worker and takes away the child's responsibility.

At Willoughby House, toughness and courage are issues of personal risk-taking, honesty, and integrity. Caring gestures among the staff and the kids are daily occurrences, and expressions of feeling are recognized as the energy that makes it all come together. The familiar signs of stress and burnout are rare indeed. I like caring, I like being cared about, and I like working in a climate where these values are held and openly expressed.

Over the past six months, I've become increasingly aware of my own personal boundaries. I've made a commitment to be honest with myself and with others, but this doesn't mean that everybody has access to my personal space. Until I began to look at this issue with Charlotte, I had no idea how much I allowed people — particularly kids — to invade my physical, psychological, and spiritual sense of being.

Since I never knew where my boundaries were from one moment to the next, I was never able to give kids a clear and consistent message. I used to wonder why I avoided or resented certain kids and why I started backing off in relationships after an initial open engagement. With little awareness or respect for boundaries, I had kids who wanted to be with me in every moment, others who wanted access to my personal life, the 'cling-ons' who needed constant physical contact, and the 'aggressors' who pushed and shoved their way into my attention. Not knowing when to say yes and when to say no, I vacillated between resentment and acceptance with expectations that were always a mystery to me and everyone else.

It seemed like such a peripheral issue at the time but, looking back, I'm not sure how I survived with such ambiguity. No wonder I was unclear in my self-focus. My self had no form or protection; it just spilled over and retreated like a jellyfish in a storm.

In determining my boundaries, I've found it better to start at a distance and move closer rather than the other way around. For me, this is a gesture of self-respect, and I believe it enhances my feelings of autonomy and esteem. This doesn't mean that I'm closed or dishonest in initial encounters. On the contrary, knowing my personal boundaries makes it possible for me to be fully present and confidently accepting in relatively superficial or passing contacts.

In considering my own boundary needs, I find that I've become increasingly aware that others also have a basic need to establish some demarkation between themselves and the rest of the world.

Entering the private space of a child's room is an obvious place for respect, but asking if the youngster is interested, before offering your personal judgements or feedback, may call for considerable restraint. As a professional child care worker, it's so easy for me to violate a boy or girl's personal boundary without awareness. I'm invested with authority, granted some expert status, and provided with tools and procedures that are mysterious to the uninitiated. When I think about all the anger and resentment that kids have directed toward me over the years, I wonder how much of this rejection came from my heavy footed trespasses.

We don't confine youngsters at Willoughby House, but I've worked in programs where some form of confinement for "acting out" or dangerous behavior was part of the procedural menu. I've come to regard this, and other restrictive practices, as a *boundary* issue rather than a *freedom* issue.

I believe that many forms of therapy, supervision, and activity programming can be even more restrictive than the short-term confinement of a child to a particular physical space. On my own in a restricted area, I would be freer to make my own choices than if I were fighting to ward off a tenacious assailant of my personal world. In my view, the use of medication represents the most intrusive form of personal violation and, if any professional procedure should be constantly subjected to public scrutiny, it's this one.

On the other hand, I've been around long enough to know that restrictive procedures are a necessary part of child care practice. I've heard most of the justifying cliches: "danger to self," "danger to others," "time out from reinforcement," "teaching impulse control," "encouraging amenability to treatment," and many more. For me, any so-called restrictive practice is an attempt to prevent further boundary violations. In the case of the 'self-destructive' youngster, one part of a disintegrated person is being protected from the violations of another part. The outwardly aggressive person is restrained from trampling down the boundaries of others. As much as possible, the particular method should respect the boundary conditions of the 'offender.' To cite an obvious example, it would not be a good idea to confine a claustrophobic person in a small restricted room.

In our program, residents and staff openly discuss and work on the establishment of personal boundaries. We have exercises that are used regularly in our group sessions, and each person is encouraged to make boundary-maintenance an on-going priority in life around the house. Then, if some form of restrictive practice is being considered, this information is taken into consideration. Where this occurs frequently with a particular resident, the method may be understood, or even negotiated ahead of time. However absurd this might appear to those who insist upon 'one rule for all,' or fear that the preferred method may serve to reinforce the undesirable behaviour, I can only say that it works at Willoughby House.

I seem to be spending a lot of time thinking about restrictive practices. They created so many dilemmas for me in other programs, and I'm just beginning to realize how much they've faded into the background. It is true that it's not much of an issue with Anna Marie, but we do have kids in the program who have lengthy histories of acting-out, aggressive behavior. Like the other forms of behavioral intervention, I think the difference is more in the orientation and the intent than the procedures themselves.

By conceptualizing restrictive practices as a boundary issue, we take it out of the punitive behavioral mould and locate it within the concept of the self. I think this shift is critical. I've seen so many workers caught in the trap of "teaching the kid a lesson," explaining and justifying the escalation of the problem in learning theory terminology. The outcome is often one of two 'selves' locked in a power struggle that can be resolved only through increasing displays of force and resistance. With the boundary perspective, the 'victim' and 'villain' mentality is replaced by genuine concern for, and interest in, the experiences of all parties. This promotes a *post-facto* discussion around shared experience rather than the wagging finger of the taskmaster and the apologetic commitments of the vanquished. It allows for the expression of authentic feelings rather than the rehearsed admonishment of a trained autocrat.

With regard to the perennial issue of restrictive practices, then, I'm arguing that the orientation of the practitioner influences the use of the procedures and determines the learning context in which such procedures are applied. In my opinion, our approach facilitates learning at many levels and, more crucially, it continues to focus upon the strength of individual selves rather than the power of an artificially created restrictive environment. I'm sure that some theoretician could take me to task on these ideas but, hopefully, Charlotte and the others will respect *my* boundaries when I discuss these notions tomorrow.

The most profound lesson that I've learned during the past six months is the importance of 'staying present in the moment.' I'm still not too happy with the term, but expressions like 'concentration' or 'attention' just don't catch the essence.

Within the first few days I began to see the value of this ability and decided, with the help of Charlotte and the others, to work diligently in learning the skills and disciplining myself to practice. I'm a headsy person by nature, and most of my life has been spent floating around among the present, the past, the future, and that dreamy world of fantasy. In my training, I'm learning to invest myself fully in each one of these states, focussing upon the present whenever there's a particular task at hand. When I manage to be fully engaged in one state or another, I'm amazed how immediate, clear, and available the other states become. So when I'm invested in the present, talking with another person, or participating in a group meeting, for example, I'm able to draw upon memory and project into the future quite effortlessly. At the same time, the creative energies of my fantasy world constantly pop ideas into my head. It's like all these levels of consciousness are in constant motion and, by focussing fully on one, the others are allowed to proceed without disruption, available as needed in the overall flow of activity. I've never discussed this notion with Charlotte but, having formulated it, I know that it will make itself available at an appropriate point in our discussions — if I stay fully present, of course.

I'm also a people pleaser. By this I mean that I lose my state of presence by trying to imagine how others see me while attempting to accommodate to their expectations. Charlotte believes that this represents my basic pre-disposition to ill health. She describes it as "floating toward unknown disasters on the unrelenting tide of other people's expectations."

In order to indulge in this futile activity, I must constantly be concerned with what I just did or said, what I should do or say next, what the consequences might be for particular actions, and how others might view me when it's all over. Working as a child care worker, I'd be talking to a particular youngster while wondering if my supervisor would approve of my approach, worrying about my credibility in the eyes of the boy or girl sitting before me, fretting about the decision I made earlier that brought the whole group back from the swimming pool, and slipping into my concern about the reports that the 'Shrink' wants on his desk by the morning. Meanwhile, I try to distract myself with thoughts of going for a few beers after the shift. In this state of 'field dependency,' riddled with self doubts, seeking the acceptance and fearing the retributions of the world while attempting to escape from it all, it's quite amazing that I manage to relate to the kid at all, let alone establish a meaningful contact.

As I hear myself express it this way, it sounds like the disassociated dilemmas of a confused idiot in desperate need of integrative psychotherapy. Certainly that was an option, but I've found that learning to focus my attention, particularly staying present in the moment, is having a dramatic effect on all aspects of my life. For me, it's been a piece of one-shot therapy although, like most profound ideas, the concept is simple while the applications and implications are difficult, complex, and far reaching. With my efforts so far, I feel good and I'm confident that I won't join the child care 'burn-out brigade.' I'm gradually coming to recognize myself and to value what I see. More and more *my* standards and *my* expectations influence the way I run my life and I'm developing a sense of purpose and being that's turning old barriers into new challenges.

I also want to put together some thoughts about my supervisor, Charlotte. I know she'd cringe if I held her in any way responsible for my experience but, in my way of viewing the world, nobody has had a greater influence upon my thinking — excluding early parental teachings, of course. In spite of this, and in spite of her commitment to openness and being 'seen,' this remarkable woman remains an elusive mystery to me. I'm convinced that she is very self-aware and she displays immense honesty in the moment, but she has chosen to remain inscrutable in my presence. I'd really like to know her better, but I'm not sure how to go about it. Perhaps I'll begin by letting her know this tomorrow.

I often think back to that moment in the staff suite after Charlotte returned from the hospital. It was a moment of fragility, of reaching out, and I was so full of self-righteous indignation that I cut her off from my humanity. I wonder how many times she's reached out before in her vulnerability, only to be objectified by those who need to use her as a fortress for their own fears. I see the curiosity, the wisdom, the softness, the intellect, and the creativity, but I struggle to see the person who offers these gifts to the world. I want to know her joy, her sadness, her fears and, most of all, what she thinks of me. This isn't another field-dependent attempt to identify and match another person's expectations. In a strange way, I believe that Charlotte's experience of me will really tell me all I need to know about Charlotte.

I do have love for Charlotte and there was a time when I believed that I was *in* love with her. In the short time that we've known each other, and without the familiar charades of dancing, cocktails, and 'your place or mine,' I seem to have moved beyond romance into genuine curiosity and unadorned respect. My attraction embraces sexuality but, for one time in my life, this is not the primary driving force. At this point, I have no intention to pursue a relationship with Charlotte beyond the context of my work at Willoughby House but there is every possibility that Charlotte will step enchantingly into center stage when I turn my spotlights on fantasy-time.

Before concluding my deliberations, I want to give some general thought to the future of my chosen profession. I no longer want to move on to acquire some other professional label but, unless I follow in the isolated footsteps of Charlotte, the opportunities in Child and Youth Care seem dismally limited. My question is whether anything can be done to broaden these horizons or whether we wait for our destiny to be determined by our lords and masters? Then, I wonder how a profession that refuses to create its own dreams and develop its own purposes can ever convince sceptical and disenchanted youngsters of the benefits of personal responsibility and self-determination?

As I see it, Child and Youth Care must develop on the basis of its own experience. Logically, this cannot occur unless the experience of child care is brought into awareness, documented, and shared. At the most fundamental level, child and youth care workers must begin by valuing their individual experience and subjecting it to personal reflection and analysis. Unfortunately, most of my colleagues seem to invalidate their own direct experience while upholding the attitudes and orientations of the none 'authoritarian' professions. So, knowing *about* children becomes more revered than knowing children. Working with the sterile prescriptions of a treatment plan designed by some third party professional seems to provide a more compelling template for action than anything that is simply known and understood through a relationship that endures the slings and arrows of daily encounters.

I used to think that our dismissal of personal experience came from a place of humility, reinforced by the vested interests of the other professions and the disinterest of administrators or policy makers. I now believe that it comes out of fear. The fear is that of a person who arrives late at a party and spends the entire evening in silence because the other guests all *seem* to know what they're talking about. The party is a tedious bore and the newcomer, who could bring new life and perspectives to the gathering, decides to emulate and hide behind the empty gestures of the others rather than take the risk of being seen. Well, it's time for me to acknowledge my boredom and speak up or leave the festivities.

I know that the child care experience is valued and shared in some quarters. At clandestine gatherings in bars and in the back rooms of conferences where they gather to hear from other professions, Child and Youth Care practitioners discuss their frustrations with Johnny's resistance, their joy around Mary's graduation, and their fear of Frank's aggression. They don't really believe Dr. Brown's diagnosis or that their Director's decision to close out two child care positions to hire another assessment psychologist is in the best interest of the kids . . . but what can they do about it?

I've heard this kind of stuff for years. I joined the local Child Care Association and served on its Executive for two years in the hope of participating in change, but there was no apparent interest in establishing the unique identity of child care through the examination of experience. For the most part, people wanted to challenge their own agencies or protect themselves and maintain the status quo through union-type activities. I'm not questioning the legitimacy of those objectives, but I guess I was looking for something different.

Of course, child and youth care workers have not been actively supported in any quest to build a sense of identity from direct and shared experience. In most agencies, few opportunities are provided for the expression of the direct line experience. In many cases, line workers are expected to follow the directions of their 'superiors' in keeping the kids in line while the 'real' objectives of the program are being pursued. Caught in the seductive exhortation of a 'we're here to be with the kids' mentality, time taken for discussion and reflection is more likely to induce guilt than excitement.

Nor have other professions gone out of their way to support the development of yet another group of expert helpers. With the ongoing battles among social work, psychiatry, and psychology, it's hardly surprising that their interest in child care is primarily one of establishing it as a sub-strata of paraprofessional support for their own particular objectives. I've worked on many multi-disciplinary teams and participated in the process of devaluing and dismissing the child care perspective in the interests of some perverse standard of professional sophistication. My thoughts seem bitter, but I must acknowledge my own shame.

Since child and youth care is rarely valued, shared, documented, and reflected upon, much of what appears in the literature can be discounted as speculative or ephemeral. Generally, the authors speak *about* Child and Youth Care rather *from* Child and Youth Care. While I subscribe to the major journals, I usually glance through each issue and moan to myself about the lack of contributions from practitioners. When my article on multi-disciplinary teams was published last year, it was the only contribution from a front line worker in the entire issue.

It's not just because child and youth care workers don't wish to write, or even that they're inhibited in this form of expression — although both factors do apply to some degree. I believe that part of the problem stems from the fact that there's no standard acceptable format for capturing the experience of child and youth care within the framework of a manuscript. Psychologists have this down to a fine art. They can take the most absurd and irrelevant piece of trivia, grind it through their patented formatting machine and, lo and behold, out pops another article for yet another journal. Psychiatrists seem to take great delight in upholding and debunking their revered notions in articles that can only be read by an initiate armed with a copy of the DSM-III. Social workers have been writing social histories for as long as children have been wetting the bed and their model of casework offers another 'fill in the words' opportunity.

Child and Youth Care is currently generating raw experience, and it takes considerable courage to put words around the personal. On the other hand, the attempts that child and youth care workers have made to filter such experiences through the standard formats of the other professions fail to capture the spirit of how it is to spend eight hours a day in face-to-face interaction with troubled kids.

If we could only celebrate and value who we are and what we do, we might be able to generate the necessary courage. I attended a public seminar two years ago that offered me some encouragement to write. A school principal and a child psychiatrist gave brief and highly professional presentations on their work. Then a Child and Youth Care worker from a local correctional facility talked about what happened during his shift on the previous day. He wasn't particularly articulate or eloquent, but he described real kids and real events that came to life through his own spirit of caring, commitment, and humour. His words were not precise and, at times, he stumbled in his efforts to communicate his thoughts, but his energy was infectious and his sincerity was profound. He had the audience spellbound. As in all great communication, particularly in the arts, people were captivated because they were somehow moved to make contact with life—with their own lives.

This is the way to communicate the world of Child and Youth Care. We all sense the child within us and, through this, we can reach out to understand and communicate with kids in trouble and with those adults who choose to work with them. If we can begin this way, the models, theories, and practices will take care of themselves. Perhaps we can establish the only profession dedicated to the sharing and dissemination of information and experience, rather than the protection of exclusivity.

A Final "Academic" Word from Tony

I participated in Paul's group evaluation yesterday. As always there was a full staff turnout and, as always, we found ourselves involved in a very special human experience. Paul had invited Anna Marie to attend and, although she didn't say much, she was obviously there for him. His openness in self-reflection was appreciated by the others, although there was general agreement that he continues to be unforgiving of himself at times. I think Anna Marie summed it up in her brief comment: "Paul is learning to love."

In my own mind, I went back to my early years as a child care worker. Now I've taken on the label of 'psychologist' but, like the inimitable supervisor at Willoughby House, I have every intention of re-establishing my identity as a child care practitioner — or child and youth care practitioner in current terminology. What I learned in child care is still at the core of my work. For me it was not the experiential stepping stone to psychology. In my frame, psychology has added new dimensions to my work with kids and families but, armed with whatever I've taken, I'll return to the fascinating world of child care practice. I know at least one person who understands.

"Act before you think." This was one of the many maddening little cliches that Charlotte used to throw at me in the old days. With my sense of reason and rationality under attack, I'd rush to find empirical support for my logical and traditional way of viewing the world. It was this search for support that first prompted me to read psychology and, eventually, to leave child care and enroll in graduate school.

By that time, it had occurred to me that these dandy little one-liners from my supervisor had some inherent value beyond my defensive frenzy of activity. I now realize that most of our 'taken for granted' notions are only as profound as their converse form, but that's another story. In this particular instance, Charlotte was inviting me to consider the idea that self-examination and discovery is a

process of observing the 'self' in action. At a broader level this also
is compatible with her preference for the cerebral realms of theory
and philosophy to follow experience, rather than vice-versa.

At first, I considered this approach to be perverse, or even dangerous, and it took almost a year for me to appreciate the learning
potential that it carried. When I entered graduate school, the wisdom of her teachings became painfully apparent. In the face of the
traditional linear thinking and the regurgitation of time-honored
models and rituals of the Department of Psychology, I decided to
learn as much as I could while jumping through the proverbial
hoops. Meanwhile, I entertained myself with some of Charlotte's
writings, combined with a weekly telephone call.

True to the wisdom that counter-positions end up incorporating
each other, it dawned on me, after graduation of course, that my
schizophrenic stance was both unnecessary and unwise. On reflection, I was able to see how Charlotte's perspective could be incorporated into more traditional paradigms. Even more exciting was
the discovery that what she was saying was actually 'predicting'
empirical developments.

I share these thoughts because, over the years, I've observed all
kinds of people struggling to package Charlotte's ideas and beliefs
into some form that can be summarily labeled and dismissed. The
'humanistic' label of the sixties became the 'human potential'
movement of the seventies, and now the term 'New Age' has been
coined by our logical positivist friends to describe yet another fad of
"non-scientific hogwash." The 'truth' is that many of the concepts
found in humanistic psychology have been evolving for a very long
time, and Charlotte has created her own particular thoughts within a
well-established tradition.

Even in the so-called 'pure' sciences many of the old linear
models have given way to ideas that turn our cause-effect logic out
on its ear. In astro-physics, the comprehension of curved space and
the anatomy of black holes demand a brand of logic that would send
most social scientists clamouring for membership in the 'Flat Earth
Society.' In physics, the replacement of particle theories by 'wave'
theories has prompted Capra and others to point out how western
scientific concepts are coming to look suspiciously like the notions
of eastern 'mysticism.' Closer to home neurologists, like Karl Pri-

bram have alienated their colleagues with "holographic" models of the brain, and scientific philosophers like David Bohm have suggested that, in the final analysis "we are the totality of our meanings." Amazing as these ideas might appear to the struggling social scientist, they are not radical to psychologists familiar with the work of contributors like Gregory Bateson, Fritz Perls, Alfred Schutz, or Edmond Husserl.

I want to make this point because the experience of child care is commonly dismissed as "subjective" and therefore "unscientific." This patronizing perspective is often assumed by other professionals who claim to have learned the scientific method, even though what they have learned may have been totally trashed by the scientists they purport to emulate. The common feature that links Charlotte with the scientists and philosophers mentioned is an underlying belief that, ultimately, all knowledge springs from, and returns to, the human psyche in the world of everyday experience. Only when this is fully appreciated will we abandon our fragmented view of ourselves and our world to discover the only vehicle for the integration of knowledge—ourselves. Within our own professional area, this perspective is most clearly represented by the holistic thinkers and practitioners and the potentials most observable through the work of psychobiologists, health researchers, and practitioners working with the mind-body-spirit paradigm.

Having said all this, I still hold to the view that the apparent gulf between empirical psychology and the perspectives offered by contributors like Charlotte is not as wide as it might seem. As I allow the psychologist within me to talk to the child care worker within me, I find that, without interference from outside 'interests,' the communication is generally open and friendly without either party attempting to dominate the other. I find the integration to be both fascinating and comforting.

Recently, I re-read Erving Goffman's (1961) book *Asylums* and made an immediate connection between his analysis of the self-management of patients in a mental hospital and the efforts of Willoughby House staff to encourage self-expression among the residents. Beyond the brilliance of Goffman as a contributor, the whole 'symbolic interactionist' tradition in social psychology has incorporated and elaborated a view of the self quite similar to the one expounded by Charlotte and her colleagues. This springs from the early ideas of writers like Charles Horton Cooley and George Herbert Mead and the practices of clinicians such as Harry Stack Sullivan. Interestingly, their perspectives have been largely ignored by researchers on the grounds that the concepts and theories don't lend themselves to traditional 'scientific methodologies.'

While the tradition of symbolic interaction established the centrality of the Self in human affairs and focussed attention upon our constant search for meaning, it fell short of Charlotte's formulations in not dealing with the issues of cognition or motivation in human activity. On the other hand, mainstream experimental psychology continues to examine the Self as a 'process of thinking' that is driven by a specific set of needs or motives. Self theorists such as Coopersmith, Raimy, and Rosenberg have identified such self needs as 'esteem,' 'autonomy,' and 'consistency' and these blend well with the picture of unique human beings striving to discover and develop a sense of self that is 'known,' worthwhile, and in charge of its own destiny. From here, notions like bringing the self present, establishing its cognitive and interpersonal boundaries, and taking full responsibility for actions are simple extrapolations.

The idea that we each create our own world in our own ways is embedded in the relativistic and existential branches of philosophy. In psychology, it is well reflected in the work of George Kelly and his creation of Personal Construct Theory. His idea that we go through life constantly generating hypotheses from our perceptions and testing them back in the laboratory of personal experience simply makes sense to me. In fact, one of the few psychological tests that I use these days is the 'Repertory Grid' developed from Kelly's work. The other instrument I like is a 'locus of control' measure, originally developed by a guy with the misfortune to inherit the name of Rotter. This operates from the familiar humanistic principle that people have the potential to experience themselves as being in charge of their lives.

In my graduate school days, the branch of cognitive psychology that most drew my attention was the investigation of something called Intrinsic Motivation. If there was ever an empirical research tradition to support the humanistic notions of personal experience and free will, this seemed to be it. Represented by the work of

Edward Deci, a plethora of laboratory and field experiments began to establish a fundamental difference between behavior in response to external 'cues' or 'reinforcers' and actions undertaken for 'self'-related reasons. Furthermore, the evidence suggests that these two forms of 'motivation' operate in opposition to one another. In experiment after experiment, it was demonstrated that people who were offered external rewards for doing things that they would choose to do anyway *lost* interest in the activity once the rewards were withheld. The same effects were noted for the use of sanctions, threats, and good old surveillance. The more compelling these external contingencies, the more dramatic the effect. In other words the external 'reasons' undermined the individual's sense of choice, or intrinsic motivation. In so many ways, this type of theory and research support the self-determination ideas of the humanistic school as well as Charlotte's well-aired concerns about behavior modification. For me, it helps to explain why many child care programs appear to lose their 'influence' when the kids move on.

In my final year at the University, I uncovered masses of material supporting a strong connection between a person's sense of self and his or her overall state of health and well-being. Autonomy and esteem were the most common correlates to be examined, but 'saliency' and 'elaboration' were noted as empirical representations of what we call "presence" and "discovery."

In the case of 'discovery' however, we are probably operating from an assumption that has never really gained acceptance in mainstream psychology. For the most part, psychologists operate from the premise that the Self is formed as we construct a view of who we are through social interaction. Charlotte, on the other hand, works from a belief that the essence of who we are is already there and that our self 'concept' is a mere approximation, while our struggle to 'understand' is a process of self-discovery.

To posit the idea of an essence or spirit is to commit an unforgivable scientific heresy. Such assumptions often lie behind the formulations of humanistic thinkers, however, even though the tradition has its roots in the often ungodly philosophy of existentialism. From my perspective, the important characteristic of this orientation is the translation of certain beliefs into values—another scientific contaminant. As a humanist, for example, I am interested in how an individual manages to attain a sense of autonomy or esteem. If these are acquired and maintained through the control, depreciation, or degradation of others, then my human potential values are offended since both victor and vanquished remain in an arrested growth pattern. As a student of human behavior, I can accept that some people, perhaps even most people, do operate this way. In other words my values make me no less of a scientist. I would also argue that my values are not a morality to be imposed on the world, since I ask only the freedom of my own beliefs. The irony is that, in my opinion, most of the oppressive moral orders emerge from the more pure, 'scientific' assumption of a black and white reality.

Many practitioners and clinicians are less skeptical than their empirical colleagues about the existence of life beyond the 'reality' of observable phenomena. Still more openly accept the idea that explanations for behavior must account for the unique configurations of personal experience. When I left graduate school, I took Charlotte's advice and spent a year studying the contributions of humanistic practitioners. While they differed in many of their beliefs and practices, the ones I chose shared a basic curiosity about the uniqueness of individual experience and a belief in the interconnectedness of all human experience.

Virginia Satir will always stand out in my mind as a quintessential contributor to the humanistic school of thought. As a pioneer in the fields of family therapy and personal growth, she influenced many practitioners in the sixties and seventies to actually make basic human contact with their clients or patients. As a teacher and facilitator, she helped to carve out the vital link between personal growth and world peace.

Erving and Miriam Polster are inimitable clinicians who have continued to extrapolate and integrate the work of Fritz Perls and the early Gestalt therapists. It is clear from all they say and write that the essential ingredient of life is reflected in our ongoing curiosity about ourselves and others in a world that can make sense only when each individual experience contacts some universal theme through the association of two or more individuals. From their work, I began to understand the importance of the small details of everyday experience that form the bases of our self-view and worldview. Through this recognition, I have taken a far more intense interest in the lives of the people I work with and the quality of my contacts with them has changed dramatically.

Bennet Wong and Jock McKeen are practitioners who co-direct a very unique learning centre on Gabriola Island in British Columbia, Canada. Combining humanistic methodologies with traditional Chinese medicine in a group setting, they have accumulated masses of experiential evidence to support their humanistic-structuralist philosophy. For many years, they have used their own relationship as a living 'laboratory' of human growth and development. It shows in their presence, in their lives, and in their work. They persistently demonstrate the tremendous power of basic human resources brought together through the skillful integration of caring, commitment, and courage.

Neurolinguistic programming was one of the few humanistic methodologies to capture the interest of my old mentors at the University. With its roots in the ideas of Gregory Bateson and moulded into shape by Grinder and Bandler, this approach has been embraced by clinicians in many parts of the world. One of the reasons for this wide acceptance is that N.L.P. combines the wisdom of humanism with the empirical designs of learning and cognitive psychology to produce a methodology designed to liberate the human will. Given the polemics and divisions that these arenas traditionally offer one another, this is no mean achievement.

I mention these examples because they are part of my history. Obviously, there are many more connections between traditional psychology and the beliefs and methodologies of Willoughby House. My own project is to work toward increased understanding and integration. It seems to me that very few of the ideas and practices I mention have been carefully examined for their applicability in child care practice. Where this has happened, it has usually been through other professionals invested in the belief that child care workers should not do 'therapy.' In my book, these things are not franchised packages to be used only by those who have paid the prescribed fees. They are part of the common stock of knowledge, available to all who accept responsibility for their actions.

With the exception of Wong and McKeen, none of the practitioners I mention here have applied their talents directly to the field of child and youth care. I am sad about this because I believe that their perspectives and experience could do much to free our profession from its developmental moratorium. We have already embraced the theories of Maslow, Erikson, Bettelheim and Piaget. We have incorporated the humanity of Trieschman, Bettelheim, Redl, and Maier. Now it's time to move beyond the hand-me-down models and practices of the psychotherapists and the behavior modifiers to create something that is distinctly and uniquely child and youth care. Then, to echo Paul's sentiments, let's put it out there for all who care about kids . . . and *themselves*, of course.

Tony's Selected Annotated Bibliography

PHILOSOPHY

Austin, D., & Halpin, W. (1987). Seeing "I" to "I": A Phenomenological Analysis of the Caring Relationship. *Journal of Child Care*. 3 (3).

> -working from the philosophy of Edmund Husserl, this article provides a short stimulating introduction to the application of phenomenology to relationships in child care.

Austin, D., & Halpin, W. (1988). The Embodiment of Knowledge: A Phenomenological Approach to Child Care. *Journal of Child Care*. The Trieschman Center Issue.

> -this article provides a fuller perspective on the applications of phenomenology than the previously cited article by the same authors. Written specifically for child care practitioners, it can be taken as an interesting viewpoint or as a way into a more detailed study of this philosophy.

Bateson, G. (1972). *Steps to an Ecology of Mind.* New York: Ballantine Books.

> -any student of the relativist-humanist perspective should be familiar with the contributions of Gregory Bateson. In this particular book, Bateson looks at the integration of all knowledge within the elaborate frameworks we create for ourselves. For the reader looking for a challenge, this book is sheer joy. It is also profound.

Bohm, D. (1985). *Unfolding Meaning*. (Edited by David Factor.) Foundation House Publications.

-an introduction to one of the most original scientific thinkers of our time. This book is actually an edited transcript of a weekend seminar. As such, it is easier reading than the written works of Professor Bohm. It is still a challenge to wrestle with some of the ideas but well worth the effort. Those who wish to plunge in at the deep end are referred to Bohm's revolutionary text, *Wholeness and the Implicate Order*. Ark Paperbacks, 1980.

Capra, F. (1983). *The Tao of Physics*. Flamingo Books.

-a very readable and authoritative exploration of the connections between western physics and eastern mysticism. It is an excellent guide for anyone struggling to understand holistic thinking and theoretical integration.

Husserl, E. (1964). *The idea of Phenomenology*, translated by William Alston and George Nakhnikian. The Hague: Martinus Nijhoff.

-along with Alfred Schutz, Edmund Husserl is synonymous with the tradition of phenomenology. Of particular relevance to the field of child care is the perspective offered for an understanding of relationships. This is not handed over to the reader on a plate but, once the menu has been understood and appreciated, the appetite is well served.

Kundera, M. (1985). *The Unbearable Lightness of Being*. New York: Harper & Row.

-this is a brilliant novel that teaches through the intellect and the senses.

Schutz, A., & Luckman, L. (1974). *The structures of the Life World.* London: Heinmann.

-a classic contribution to the field of 'phenomenology,' primarily containing the work of Alfred Schutz. The text describes how we construct a view of the world through our ongoing experience in everyday life. This is not easy reading for those not used to the grammar of philosophy but it's well within the reach of those who are prepared to make the effort.

Wilber, K. (1982). *The Holographic Paradigm and other paradoxes.* Boston: New Science Library.

-a startling book for those who are entrenched in a traditional view of scientific thinking. In this book Ken Wilber has put together some of the most dramatic new ideas from highly credible contributors in various fields of scientific endeavour. For child care workers, this book is bound to raise questions about the concepts and models that have been incorporated into everyday practice.

Winch, P. (1958). *The Idea of a Social Science and its Relation to Philosophy.* New York: Humanities Press.

-a short book for the serious student of social philosophy. Some familiarity with the works of Wittgenstein, J.S. Mill, and Max Weber would be helpful.

Woollam, R.H. (1985). *On Choosing—with a Quiet Mind.* Duncan, B.C. Canada: Unica Publishing Company Ltd.

-a wonderful book for anyone prepared to challenge his or her orientation to everyday life. Ray Woollam invites his readers to acknowledge the choices they make and free themselves from the entrapment of their worlds through the resources of their own imagination. This book is fun, highly readable and very thought-provoking.

PSYCHOTHERAPY

Ashby Willis, T. (1982). *Basic Processes in Helping Relationship.*
New York: Academic Press.

-this 'text book' brings together some of the most critical research findings in the area of 'helping' relationships. Although
some of the contributions are presented in a typical research
format, the uninitiated reader can still understand the basic
themes and the essential findings. The chances are that most
child care practitioners will be quite surprised at what research
actually has to say to people who set out to help others.

Bandler, R., & Grinder, J. (1979). *Frogs into Princes.* Real People
Press.

-an introduction to Neuro Linguistic Programming. This far
reaching perspective offers the compelling idea that we can
actually take charge of our own experiences and make them
what we want them to be. It is written in a style that will
challenge the most sceptical and 'unprepared' reader.

Bandler, R., & Grinder, J. (1982). *Reframing.* Edited by Steve
Andreas and Connie Andreas. Real People Press.

-another volume in the N.L.P. series. This one deals with one
of the most important methods introduced in the *Frogs into
Princes* text. Reframing is a wonderfully empowering cognitive strategy that make it possible for us to change our relationships with the world through transformations of meaning.
Even for practitioners who don't intent to follow the methodology of N.L.P., the ideas in this book have many practical and
personal applications.

Bugental, J. (1987). *The Art of the Psychotherapist.* New York: Norton & Company.

-a very informative and instructive account of the existential position in psychotherapy. It offers guidance to those who wish to develop their skills as well as the insights and experiences of a master of the art.

Button, E. (1985). *Personal Construct Theory & Mental Health.* Cambridge: Brookline Books.

-a text that introduces the essential concepts of George Kelly and examines their application across the arena of mental health. This is definitely a text book intended for the serious student of cognitive psychology.

Chapman, A.H. (1978). *The Treatment Techniques of Harry Stack Sullivan.* New York: Brunner/Mazel.

-a book for the serious reader but, laced with therapist-patient dialogue, it is both entertaining and instructive. There is little doubt that Sullivan is the most influential 'unknown' psychiatrist of the century who "secretly dominates American Psychiatry."

Erikson, E. (1963). *Childhood and Society.* New York: Norton & Company.

-this is simply a seminal work that should be read by all child care practitioners.

Kottler, J. (1986). *On Being a Therapist.* San Francisco: Jossey-Bass.

-one of the few books on psychotherapy that incorporates the direct subjective experience of the therapist. Written for the practicing psychotherapist, this book is good reading for anyone seriously interested in the lives of people who work with people.

Perls, F. Hefferline, R., & Goodman, P. (1951). *Gestalt Therapy* New York: Julian Press.

-this is the definitive work and compulsory reading for any person claiming to have considered the gestalt perspective.

Polster, E. (1987). *Every Person's Life is Worth a Novel*. New York: Norton & Company.

-a very articulate and imaginative perspective that relates the world of the psychotherapist to the world of the novelist. This book can be read and appreciated by the casual reader, the serious student and the seasoned practitioner. It is a wonderful reminder of the rich and fascinating patterns woven into all of our lives.

Polster, E., & Polster, M. (1974). *Gestalt Therapy Integrated*. New York: Brunner/Mazel.

-a developmental extrapolation of the original work of Fritz Perls and his colleagues. In this volume, the Polsters bring their own originality into the tradition of Gestalt Therapy. This is a first class handbook for any practitioner intent upon incorporating gestalt techniques into his or her practices.

Robbins, A. (1986). *Unlimited Power*. New York: Fawcett Columbine.

-this is one of the most popular self development books ever published. It also outlines the framework of Neuro Linguistic Programming. It is easy to read and understand.

Rothenberg, A. (1988). *The Creative Process of Psychotherapy*. New York: Norton & Company.

-relationships are vehicles for creativity. In the art of psychotherapy, the creative processes are those that bring life to the experience while the discipline ensures its fundamental purpose. If child care can ever bring these two elements together it will truly have a foundation for professional practice. This is a 'sophisticated' book that should appeal to those interested in creative new models and methodologies.

THE SELF

Deikman, A. (1982). *The Observing Self*. Boston: Beacon Press.

-a provocative little book for those interested in the theme of blending western 'science' with eastern 'mysticism.' Although it is framed within the tradition of psychotherapy, it should also appeal to readers concerned with personal 'growth.'

Goffman, E. (1959). *The Presentation of Self in Everyday Life*. New York: Doubleday Anchor Books.

-this acclaimed work described how people *present* particular images of themselves to others. It deals with the art of disguising and masking the authentic self as a strategy for 'survival' in social interaction. In another book, *Asylums* (1961, Anchor Books), Goffman describes how 'self management' occurs within the context of a mental hospital. Even to this day, it provides a dramatic frame of reference for child care practitioners working in residential settings.

Rosenberg, M. (1979). *Conceiving the Self*. New York: Basic Books Inc.

-a text book by design but one of the best general theories of the self available in the realm of empirical psychology. For the reader unfamiliar with the literature this book will be a challenge but it is certainly understandable. On completion even the 'neophyte' will understand how people come to form a 'concept' of who they are.

RELATIONSHIPS

Fewster, G. (1987). The Paradoxical Journey: Some Thoughts on Relating to Children. *The Journal of Child Care*. 3 (3).

>   -a radical look at adult/child relationships challenging some of our more comfortable and accepted notions. This article offers a point of departure for practitioners who want to reconstruct their thinking and reconsider their practices.

McKeen, J., & Wong, B. (1987). To Be..Love-ing . . . To Be. *Journal of Child Care* 3 (3).

>   -one of the few attempts to deal boldly with the issue of love within the context of relationships. Written specifically for child and youth care workers, it offers an invaluable perspective on this much abused topic.

Satir, V. (1976). *Making Contact*. Celestial Arts.

>   -in her own inimitable style Virginia Satir offers us the profound by teaching us the simple. On reading this small volume the reader is introduced to things already 'known' but rarely seen and understood. This is the kind of book that can stay on your desk to be read many times over.

HUMAN DEVELOPMENT

Kagan, J. (1984). *The Nature of the Child*. New York: Basic Books, Inc.

>   -probably the best contribution to developmental psychology since Piaget. If only one book is to be read on this topic this might well be the one to consider.

Maier, H. (1988). *Three Theories of Child Development*. New York: University Press of America. (Also NY: Harper & Row, 1978).

> -first class review by an internationally respected child care worker. This book examines the contributions of theorists Jean Piaget, Erik Erikson and Robert Sears. What more could be asked for?

Piaget, J. (1969). *The Psychology of the Child*. New York: Basic Books.

> -no child and youth care worker can claim to be a professional without a clear understanding of the work of Jean Piaget. This book offers the principal concepts and theories.

GENERAL CHILD CARE

Axline, V. (1964). *Dibs in search of self*. New York: Ballantine Books.

> -the only book on child care to hit the best seller lists in North America. This book is still an entertaining and relevant little classic.

Krueger, M. (1987). *Floating*. Washington: Child Welfare League of America.

> -one of the few attempts to capture the spirit of child and youth care in a narrative form. Written by a major contributor to the field, this book captures the attention and the heart.

Maier, H. (1987). *Developmental Group Care of Children and Youth*. New York: The Haworth Press.

> -an overview of the ideas and methods generated by the one and only Henry Maier. If you have only the money to buy, or the time to read, one book, you may decide that this is the one. It is a first class handbook for the busy practitioner.

Paul, J. & Paul, M. (1987). *If You Really Loved Me . . .* CompCare
  Publishers.

> -offered as a general guide for parents, this book deals sensi-
> bly and creatively with the management of conflict in adult/
> child relationships. It demonstrates how child and youth care
> can be a loving process that respects both self and other.

Trieschman, A., Whittaker, J., & Brendtro, L. (1969). *The Other
  23 Hours.* Chicago: Aldine.

> -if you are in the field of child and youth care and you have not
> read this book, you are a rare specimen. Please rectify this
> problem immediately.